I love this book. It is simple, practical, a[...] on asking good questions is worth the price of the whole book. If you're looking for a way to have more meaningful spiritual conversations with people, *How to Talk about Jesus without Looking like an Idiot* will do exactly as the title suggests.

> SEAN McDOWELL, PhD, professor at Biola University, popular YouTuber, and the author or editor of over twenty books, including *A Rebel's Manifesto*

With his unique blend of humour, wit, and incisive analysis, Andy helps us navigate the opportunities and pitfalls of sharing faith today. This accessible book is a must-read for all Christians who want to talk about Jesus with greater confidence and winsomeness.

> AMY ORR-EWING, PhD, author, speaker, and theologian

We all want to live in such a way as believers that our words and our lives match so that our walk is the same as our talk. But the subject where we see the greatest gap between what Christians *say* is vital and how their lives *reflect* that is evangelism. That's why Andy Bannister's book is so refreshing. His humor is infectious, but don't let it fool you. There is a wealth of wisdom and insight in these pages, with some of the most honest, practical, and helpful tools I've seen in a book on evangelism. Read it and laugh at Andy's wit, then put his teaching into practice. The Good News in Jesus is too good not to tell, and Andy will help you.

> ED STETZER, PhD, Wheaton College

Having worked with Andy Bannister on various evangelistic events for years, I can confidently say that he knows how to talk about Jesus without looking like an idiot. In this book, he teaches the rest of us how to do the same. Besides being highly entertaining, this book is an accessible treasure trove of real-world insight and practical tips. If you love Jesus and want to share that love naturally and effectively with others, this is a must-read and reread!

ANDY STEIGER, PhD, founder and president of Apologetics Canada and author of *Reclaimed*

There is an idiom we use in the UK, "to throw the kitchen sink" at something. It means to try everything; exhaust all energy and resources in order to achieve something or to solve a problem. . . . Andy "throws the kitchen sink" into evangelism and apologetics. . . . Once again Andy is giving his very best to what matters most to him, helping people like you and me introduce others to Jesus. I honestly can't recommend this book highly enough. . . . There are over three hundred books on evangelism and apologetics around my study, and as a resource to the church, I'd confidently put this in the top five. From new Christians to seasoned pilgrims, this is a wonderfully emotive and empowering read.

MITCH CROWN, evangelist/CEO at Crown Jesus Ministries, Ireland

Not for the first time, Andy Bannister has written a book which is as witty as it is accessible. His modest tone and laconic style undergird a razor-sharp mind and robust intellect. It's always a pleasure to read his work and to feel excited about where this book may end up.

ANDY KIND, comedian and author

Plastic dinosaurs, *The Princess Bride*, airborne deck-chairs—this how-to on evangelism has it all. But don't let the gentle humour fool you. Andy has produced an accessible, insightful, and culturally savvy text on sharing the gospel in our increasingly hostile, post-Christian setting. But it's not just how he, with all his years of experience, can do that—but how we can too. Andy demonstrates a love for the lost and a love for the people of God as they navigate these tough times in which gospel fruit seems less likely and the chance of being viewed as a bigot or weirdo more likely. Most of all, he shows a love for Jesus that drives the desire to evangelise in the first place. This book takes modern objections to the gospel seriously yet demonstrates how, through clear strategies, biblical instruction, and helpful examples, these objections can be met. Written in plainspeak, it offers compelling reasons as to why, when done thoughtfully, the good news "hits different" in a culture which thinks it knows why it has left Christianity behind yet can't come up with a satisfying alternative.

STEPHEN McALPINE, Director of Cultural Engagement for City to City Australia

With humor, wit, and an unsinkable sense of spiritual buoyancy, Andy Bannister unpacks practical ways to share your faith with the people around you, and he peppers these pages with real-life stories that bring his principles to life. This book will help launch you on the unparalleled adventure of influencing others for Christ.

MARK MITTELBERG, author of *Contagious Faith* and executive director of the Lee Strobel Center for Evangelism and Applied Apologetics at Colorado Christian University

In my experience, telling other people about Jesus is one of the greatest causes of anxiety for the average Christian. But fear not, help is at hand. Delivered with Andy's inimitable sense of humour, this book is a brilliant guide to sharing your faith naturally and confidently. It won't magically turn you into a super evangelist (as Andy explains, they don't really exist in real life), but it will help you to face your fears, start conversations, and simply talk to people about Jesus . . . without looking like an idiot.

JUSTIN BRIERLEY, author, broadcaster, and host of the *Unbelievable?* show

Is it fitting for evangelism to be, dare we say, enjoyable? In my experience, Christians can unintentionally take the delight out of evangelism by the way we approach it. Enter Andy Bannister, whose jovial jesting and humorous life stories, combined with a depth of knowledge and experience, demonstrate a true compassion for, *and enjoyment of*, his fellow humans. His book is overflowing with evangelistic expertise alongside well-crafted suggestions that are simple to implement and easy to remember, encouraging and empowering you to naturally share your life and faith with others.

MARY JO SHARP, assistant professor of apologetics at Houston Christian University and author of *Why I Still Believe: A Former Atheist's Reckoning with the Bad Reputation Christians Give a Good God*

How to Talk about Jesus without Looking like an Idiot

HOW TO
TALK ABOUT
JESUS
WITHOUT
LOOKING
LIKE AN
IDIOT

A PANIC-FREE GUIDE TO
HAVING NATURAL CONVERSATIONS
ABOUT YOUR FAITH

ANDY BANNISTER

TYNDALE
elevate™
ask. seek. find.

A Tyndale nonfiction imprint

Visit Tyndale online at tyndale.com.

Tyndale and Tyndale's quill logo are registered trademarks of Tyndale House Ministries. *Tyndale Elevate* and the Tyndale Elevate logo are trademarks of Tyndale House Ministries. Tyndale Elevate is a nonfiction imprint of Tyndale House Publishers, Carol Stream, Illinois.

How to Talk about Jesus without Looking like an Idiot: A Panic-Free Guide to Having Natural Conversations about Your Faith

Designed by Ron C. Kaufmann

Edited by Jonathan Schindler

Published in association with the literary agency of Mark Sweeney & Associates, Carol Stream, Illinois.

For information about special discounts for bulk purchases, please contact Tyndale House Publishers at csresponse@tyndale.com, or call 1-855-277-9400.

Library of Congress Cataloging-in-Publication Data

A catalog record for this book is available from the Library of Congress.

ISBN 978-1-4964-6239-8

Printed in the United States of America

29	28	27	26	25	24	23
7	6	5	4	3	2	1

To my wife, Astrid.

Thank you for over two decades of love, support, encouragement, and friendship (and for helping occupy the smaller members of the household whilst I took the time to write this book!).

CONTENTS

Foreword

As a new Christian working among spiritually skeptical colleagues at a major newspaper, I refrained from telling others about Jesus. I didn't want to embarrass myself. I was scared I'd get stumped by a question. I was afraid of what might happen to my career if I became known as the newsroom's "Holy Roller." The only hint I gave about my newfound faith was to decline my boss's invitation to go golfing on Sunday because I'd be at church.

Then one hectic day when everyone was losing their tempers because of all the breaking news, my boss came over to my desk. "Strobel, how did you get through the day without blowing your top?" he asked. Then, apparently suspecting a link between my behavior and church, he added, "What's this Christianity thing to you?"

I froze. Nobody had ever asked me that before. My mind raced. Maybe I could dismiss the whole thing with a joke. *Christianity? Hey, what happens in church stays in church!* Maybe I could pretend I didn't hear him over the din of the newsroom. *Yeah, it's been a crazy day. Man, look at the time! I've gotta get home to my wife!*

That's when the uninvited words of the apostle Paul coursed through my mind: "I am not ashamed of the gospel" (Romans 1:16). *Great!* I fumed. *Just want I needed—a biblical guilt trip!*

Then I made a split-second decision to take a spiritual risk. "You really want to know?" I asked. "Let's go into your office."

Behind closed doors, we talked for forty-five minutes—well, actually, I talked. I was really nervous and totally unprepared. In my own sincere but inept way, I stumbled through describing how I met Jesus and the difference he made in my life. I feared I was coming off like an idiot—but then something amazing happened.

My boss didn't laugh. He didn't make fun of me. He didn't nervously try to change the topic or make excuses to leave the room. Instead, he listened intently. By the end, he was hanging on every word.

At the same time, I felt like I was going to burst on the inside. It instantly became clear to me that nothing was as urgent or exciting as what I was doing at that very moment. I felt as if eternity were holding its breath. Emerging from his office, I was thoroughly invigorated, as if the air were carbonated. There are no words to adequately describe the thrill I felt in having been sued by God to share his message of hope with someone far from him.

Have you experienced that joy? If you want to but feel hindered by the kind of fears that prompted me to keep my mouth shut for so long, then you've picked up the perfect book. With wit and wisdom, my friend Andy Bannister will take you on a journey of discovery to help you understand how sharing Jesus with others can be natural and effective.

Through his real-world insights and compelling stories, Andy provides practical advice that you can put to use starting today. It's amazing how our fears and hesitations dissipate when we acquire simple techniques that we can weave into our everyday encounters. When we understand the keys to asking good questions, for instance, we find that conversations about Jesus can be stimulating and exciting, not scary and intimidating.

So read on with an open mind and heart. Have a highlighter handy. C'mon, you've always wanted to be a difference-maker for Christ! Here's your chance to learn and grow through Andy's godly coaching. Then make the decision that when God opens an opportunity, you'll make the choice to take a spiritual risk and share the best news on the planet.

Lee Strobel
Founding director,
Lee Strobel Center for Evangelism
and Applied Apologetics at
Colorado Christian University

CHAPTER 1

UNDERCOVER CHRISTIAN

I HAVE WORKED FOR SOME REMARKABLY strange people in my time, but none was so wonderfully and extravagantly eccentric as Professor Arthur Crump. He was my first boss and head of the psychiatry department at St. George's, the London hospital where I'd landed my first job after leaving school. When he wasn't shuffling up and down the corridors shoeless and wearing odd socks or talking lovingly to the rubber plant in his office (which for some reason was named Oswald), one of Arthur's hobbies was photography.

On one occasion, Arthur had decided it would be a capital idea to come into work before the crack of dawn, head up to the roof of the secure psychiatry ward, and take a picture of the sun rising over the river that wound through the hospital grounds. So there Arthur was at 4:00 a.m., equipped with his Nikon and a flask of coffee, and sure enough, he took some quite impressive photographs. But then disaster struck! A gust of wind blew the fire door shut, and Arthur found himself stranded on the roof. This was in the days before mobile phones, so he sat and waited for somebody to arrive who could help to release him.

About 6:00 a.m., a milk delivery driver pulled into the hospital car park. Arthur leaned over the parapet and from three storeys up boomed, "Hello, my good man, I'm stuck on the roof!" The driver ignored him, and so Arthur tried again: "I'm stuck up here on the roof! Could you find somebody to let me out?"

The driver yelled back, "Not a chance, mate. You're a raving lunatic!"

"No, no, you don't understand," Arthur shouted, "I'm actually the professor of psychiatry!"

"Yeah, mate, and I'm the queen of England!" came the reply as the driver climbed back into his truck and drove away, leaving Arthur stranded for two more hours until he was finally recognised and rescued.

For years, that story was repeated around our department to hoots of laughter, along with tales of the other strange things Arthur had done. "Olympic-level eccentric" or "Nice but *really* weird" were the kind of phrases his colleagues used to describe him.

And I was worried those same colleagues would conclude exactly the same thing about me if they knew my deepest secret— the secret I tried to hide during all my years working at St. George's. Many of my colleagues at the hospital had literal skeletons in their cupboards, whereas I had a metaphorical one. I was not the queen of England or the professor of psychiatry. But I was a Christian.

Yes, I was a Christian—and not in some vague "I'm a Christian because I was christened as a child and can remember one-and-a-half verses of 'Jerusalem'[1] from singing hymns at school" sense of the word. No, I was a Christian in the incredibly serious and committed sense. Outside of work, I was very engaged in my local church, heavily involved with youth work and other activities. If you had asked me, I would have described my faith as the most important thing in my life.

But you would have struggled to spot that *inside* work.

At work, I played a game I came to think of as Undercover Christian, which I always thought would make a great movie title and would feature Christians sneaking around trying to never let slip to their colleagues what they really believed.[2] During my Monday to Friday workweek, I would have done *anything* to avoid being outed as a Christian.

Mondays were often the worst, because then there would be the What Did You Do on the Weekend question, and occasionally I'd slip up.

"How was your weekend, Andy?"

"Oh, it was great, on Sunday morning I went to a fantastic ch— ch— ch— cheese-making seminar."

On another occasion I'd foolishly brought in a Christian book and was sitting in the staff canteen reading it as a colleague walked in.

"What's that book you're reading?" they asked.

"Which book? Oh, *this* book? *This* book? Ah, it's, well, about—look! Look out the window! My word, is that a fish? Or is it a bird?"

I think the closest I ever came to having my Christian faith

---

[1] The answer to the first verse of this peculiarly British hymn is "No, they didn't," and the answer to the second is "Fetch it yourself."

[2] When the British crime drama *Silent Witness* premiered, I confess that on first seeing the title I thought it was about Christians in the workplace. As a wit once remarked, "Many Christians are like arctic rivers—they have frozen mouths."

outed at work happened one day when I accidentally dropped a large fax machine on my foot.[3] Hopping around in agony and feeling the need to curse, but wanting to avoid swearing like a trooper, I shouted something inoffensive like "Bother!" My colleague eyed me suspiciously. "You're not one of those weird religious types who think it's wrong to swear?" she asked, narrowing her eyes. "Flipping heck, no!" I exclaimed. (As a Baptist, I thought that was pretty strong.)

Inwardly, all of this was tearing me to pieces. I spent years feeling incredibly guilty for being afraid of my Christian faith at work, for burying it away, for role-playing Undercover Christian. After all, weren't Christians supposed to be brave and fearless? I'd grown up on stories of Christian heroes from the past, like Perpetua or Dietrich Bonhoeffer, who boldly proclaimed their faith in the face of threats and even death. Meanwhile, I couldn't even face the banter around the water cooler. In the Scriptures, I would read passages like Ephesians 6, which talks about the belt of truth and the helmet of salvation. Meanwhile, my own spiritual attire seemed more akin to the flip-flops of fear, the socks of silence, and the underpants of uncertainty.

I especially struggled with the dissonance that characterised my life—the massive gap between living an active Christian life at home and at church, whilst at work I hid my light under a bowl, the bowl under a box, and the box in a locked filing cabinet stuck in a disused basement lavatory with a sign on the door saying, "Beware of the leopard!"

For six years at St. George's Hospital I played Undercover Christian—and as it eventually turned out, I was not the only

---

3 Unfortunately, it turns out that fax don't always care about your feelings.

one. At the leaving lunch that was organised when I moved on to another job, I got chatting with a woman who worked three doors down from me, and through discovering a mutual friend, we suddenly found out we were both Christians! She had also been playing Undercover Christian for the last six years, and thus I had no idea I hadn't been the only Christian in the department. I suspect there were others and that Undercover Christian wasn't a one-off movie; it was quite probably a multiseason box set.

The Foundations of Fear

So where had my nervousness about talking about my faith in Jesus at work come from? Why was it that I found it perfectly simple to talk to my colleagues about the weather, sports, or my hobbies,[4] but when it came to the most important thing in my life—my faith in Jesus—I clammed up more tightly than an oyster with lockjaw? What exactly was the problem? Looking back, I think one contributing factor was that most of my experiences or models of sharing my faith had been terribly unhelpful—or in some cases, downright terrifying.

Falling into the latter category, for example, was the time in my late teens when our church pastor had decided it would be a marvellous idea to "get the youth group involved in evangelism." (Phrases like "young and enthusiastic," "creative and energetic," and "cannon fodder" were mentioned.) And so, those of us in the youth group first tried sharing our faith by means of drama skits so painfully bad that one old lady took pity and gave us some money to go buy ice creams. Finally, we were dispatched door to door, tasked with inviting people to the Christmas service. Among

---

4 "I love collecting stamps," I once explained to a coworker. "What a brilliant hobby," she said. "Philately will get you nowhere," I replied.

the highlights of that particular adventure were trying to talk to somebody whilst their dogs snarled at us angrily ("They really are harmless and friendly when you get to know them. Grip! Wolf! Fang! Stop chewing the nice man's leg!") and knocking on a door that was opened by a four-hundred-pound man who was entirely naked except for a small purple beret.

Other examples of evangelism I had seen suffered from the opposite problem: they were far too impressive. In 1989, Billy Graham had come to the UK and spoken at Crystal Palace Athletics Stadium in London, a few miles from where I lived. The weather did what British weather normally does and rained dismally, but Billy preached his heart out whilst the rain dripped steadily off his nose—after which thousands responded and gave their lives to Christ. In the very back I sat and watched, impressed, concluding that to be effective at telling others about Jesus you had to be (a) an incredibly gifted orator and (b) waterproof.

I also found it intimidating to have one or two friends who were very clearly gifted in this way. My friend Michael, for example, seemed able to simply sneeze and people became Christians. Every time we met, he would have some remarkable new story, my favourite of which was a long-winded recounting of how he'd managed to lead his dentist to Christ whilst his dentist was performing a root canal on him.

And so, as a young Christian, it seemed patently obvious. Telling others about Jesus was for specialists. It was for professionals. And it wasn't for me.

Over the years, I have come to realise that I'm not alone in all of this. That fear of talking about our faith at work and the feeling that it isn't something for ordinary people is widespread in the church. A great many Christians are afraid of talking about

Jesus—and feel guilty, foolish, or inadequate because of this. Lots of pastors I speak to back this up, too, often telling me how difficult it can be to get people excited or engaged when it comes to sharing their faith. As one Canadian pastor put it to me, "I struggle to get volunteers for anything related to evangelism. To be honest, it's easier to find volunteers to clean the church lavatories. With a toothbrush."

The Way Ahead

Thankfully, in the twenty or so years since I worked at St. George's Hospital and played my daily game of Undercover Christian, I have learnt a lot, not least from having had the privilege of learning from dozens of Christian men and women who have figured out ways by which sharing our faith can be less frightening. And so, as the saying goes, I wish I knew *then* what I know *now*. If I had a time machine, I would love to go back and say a few things to my twenty-three-year-old self. Probably beginning with "Don't try to look cool by wearing black turtlenecks—with your complexion, you look like a small, startled badger."

More seriously, I'd want to share a few lessons with my younger self that I have learnt since then. For example, I'd want to say, "You're not alone in finding it tough to share your faith." (I really did think it was just me who was having such a hard time.) I would want to explain that telling others about Jesus doesn't have to be intimidating, not least because there are really simple, basic, and practical tools that *anybody* can use to help them do it more naturally. And above all, I would want to point out to my younger self that God really can use anybody, not just specialists, as his ambassadors.

Hopefully the twenty-three-year-old me would have listened

attentively and not died of shock at seeing his future self, because that would have caused a time paradox comparable to the plot of *Back to the Future*. But if my younger self had asked me to justify especially that last claim, I'd have said one word: "the prophet Jonah." Admittedly that's three words but hey, I've just travelled in time and you're nit-picking over things like that?

Anyway, back to Jonah. Have you ever thought what a terrible evangelist he was? God commands him to go to Nineveh, but Jonah is such a racist, he doesn't want to preach to *those* people. And when God sends him anyway, he jumps on a boat headed in quite literally the opposite direction. Only after a violent storm and a few days stuck inside a giant fish does Jonah, grudgingly, go to Nineveh, where he preaches what is, quite frankly, a rubbish sermon (and short: just five words in Hebrew!). Yet despite his cowardice, racism, and laziness, God uses Jonah to save an entire city full of people. As Glen Scrivener puts it,

> The great evangelist of the Bible is not Jonah, it's the Lord. And that's good news because by the Spirit, the Lord continues to reach out through rubbish evangelists like Jonah, like me, like you. As you seek to share your faith with others today, take heart: nothing can thwart God's gospel mission to the ends of the earth—not even you can thwart it. Because "Salvation comes from the Lord." (Jonah 2:9)[5]

I find those words deeply encouraging. Not even you or I—however rubbish evangelists or fearful we may think we are—can

5 Glen Scrivener, *Reading Between the Lines: Old Testament Daily Readings*, Volume 1 (Leyland, UK: 10Publishing, 2018), 469.

muck up God's plans. But if we let him, God can work through even us.

All that is what I would love to share with my twenty-three-year-old self. Alas, my plan to travel back in time suffers from just two flaws. First, that time travel has not yet been invented and is probably impossible. And second, that time travel has not yet been invented and is probably impossible. (Admittedly that's the same problem, but it's such a major problem, it was worth listing twice.)

However, what I decided I *could* do was write the book I wish I had been able to read back then and, in the absence of rifts or rips in the fabric of space-time, at least pass it on to people it might encourage and equip. Helping others learn to overcome their fears of sharing their faith is, in fact, what I've been doing for the last decade, as I've taught the material in this book to tens of thousands of Christians across Canada, the United States, and Europe—Christians who are not specialists, just men and women who, like you and me, would love to be able to feel they can talk about Jesus without looking like an idiot.

If any of what I've described above resonates with you—if you're nervous or fearful of speaking about your faith at work, or simply don't know how to start talking about Jesus to your friends—I hope that *How to Talk about Jesus without Looking like an Idiot* will do four things for you. First, I hope it will build some confidence (and trust me, if *I* can grow in confidence, then there is hope for *anybody*). Second, I hope it will give you some practical tools you can use in everyday conversations—not just *theory*, but actual tools you can use. Third, I hope it will get you *excited* to talk about Jesus with your friends and colleagues. Fourth, I hope it will encourage you, through the stories and examples, that God can use *you*. And I hope it will do all of those things in a friendly, funny, down-to-earth, and reassuring way. That's why I persuaded the artist who designed the cover to plaster the words "DON'T PANIC" on the front in large, friendly letters.

But when it comes to sharing our faith, many of us *do* panic. We're nervous, and we're afraid. So let's begin by asking, What *precisely* are we afraid of? Because the first step to tackling our fears about evangelism is to bring them into the light and name them.

CHAPTER 2

THE SUM OF ALL FEARS

WE LIVE IN A VERY FEAR-BASED CULTURE. So much of our politics, media, and public discourse is riven by fear, not least because fear appears to work rather well at motivating people. As a wit once remarked, "The best leaders inspire by example; when that's not an option, sheer terror works pretty well too." Our news media is full of endless stories about things we should be afraid of: climate change, pandemics, financial crashes, asteroid strikes, tortoises,[1] shark attacks, coconuts falling on you, and so on.

Statistically speaking, you are far more likely to be killed by a coconut falling on you than by a shark (not least because sharks don't tend to climb trees), which is one reason I moved to Dundee in Scotland, where we have neither sharks nor coconuts, although

---

[1] There's even a word for this: herpetophobia. And as the novelist Terry Pratchett once remarked, "Until you realise there's a tortoise stuck under your brake pedal you've never known the meaning of fear, and possibly not the meaning of 'old age' either." Terry Pratchett and Gray Jolliffe, *The Unadulterated Cat: A Campaign for Real Cats* (London: Victor Gollancz, 1989), 29.

somebody was badly injured here in 1873 when they were savaged by a haggis. So you take your risks as you find them.

All jokes aside, fear can be genuinely crippling, and fear—whether irrational or otherwise—can hold you back in all kinds of ways. For instance, until my midthirties I was afraid of flying. Not afraid in a mild "white knuckles holding onto the armrest and repenting of any sin I can possibly think of during takeoff" kind of fear, but rather the "I'm not even going to get on a plane unless you sedate me first" variety. After ten years of putting up with this nonsense, my wife finally managed to talk me into flying to the United States to visit friends. As we sat at the departure gate, my heart rate up in the 150s and my adrenaline levels in the red zone, I contemplated whether I could sneak to the washroom, find a window, and escape from the airport, leaving her to travel to New York on her own. "I think I'll just visit the lavatory," I said innocently to my wife, who, not to be fooled, replied, "Not a chance; you can use the one on the plane."

For years, my fear of flying kept me from experiencing the joys of travel, and it was only eventually overcome through a combination of watching endless air crash documentaries, lots of prayer, and talking to a friend who was a pilot. My pilot friend had some good advice. He encouraged me to be specific—to *name* my fears. Fear of flying, you see, is too general an idea, so it helps to narrow it down. "I'm afraid the wings will fall off" or "I'm afraid we'll run out of fuel and plummet to the ground like lemmings wearing concrete boots" are more specific fears, and by identifying them, we can more easily address them.

Similarly, when it comes to our fears about sharing our faith in Jesus with friends and colleagues, we need to get specific. What *precisely* is it that we're afraid of? A key step in overcoming our fears is to name them, to bring them out of the cupboard and into the light of day where they may shrivel in the sunlight. From reflecting on my own struggles as well as talking to thousands of Christians over the years, I have come to believe that there are eight common fears when it comes to sharing our faith. Let's name them one by one.

Fear of Looking like an Idiot

Let's be honest, this is the big one, isn't it? It's also the reason, presumably, why you purchased a book called *How to Talk about Jesus without Looking like an Idiot*, unless of course you received it as a Christmas present from your dear old grandmother whose gift-buying track record isn't the best. (That luminous lime green knitted cardigan last year!) But given you're on chapter 2 already, there must be something in the title that intrigues you.

None of us want to look foolish or stupid. Although, having said that, when it comes to throwing ourselves wholeheartedly into silly party games at the office Christmas social or joining in the neighbourhood parents-versus-teenagers street hockey game and ending up flat on our backs in the rosebushes, there are plenty of times when the risk of looking like a twit doesn't stop us.

So there's got to be something deeper going on than merely "I'm afraid of looking like an idiot." The same was true with my fear of flying. Anxieties about terminal velocity or metal fatigue weren't the *real* issue. I figured out the real issue was *control*. I liked to be in control, and sitting in a metal tube hurtling along at 500 mph some 30,000 feet in the air whilst trusting that the person flying the plane knew what they were doing was about as far from "control" as it was possible to be. Likewise, when it comes to the fear of looking like an idiot for sharing our faith, I think the actual, underlying fear is that we'll be unpopular or disliked by our friends and peers.

We all have a desire to be liked. It's very natural and very human. I still remember with horror the dreaded "team sports" during my schooldays. All the class would be lined up against the wall, and the two captains would alternate turns picking people for their team. Oh, the shame and embarrassment of being last, of not fitting in, because I was totally nonsporty, at least when it came to anything involving a ball, a bat, or a banjo.[2] Maybe you can remember similar situations in your own life when you very obviously didn't fit in and a sense of awkwardness sweated from every pore.

And I believe that for many of us, that's at the heart of our fears about sharing our faith. *What if talking about Jesus means I don't fit in to the group as I did before? What if I risk being excluded or am somehow no longer accepted in the way I once was?* One of the most pervasive ideologies of our age is Performance Based Acceptance, the toxic idea that to be accepted, we need to perform a certain way. Our culture encourages the idea that the things that matter are our grades, our salary, our output, our looks, our conformity to the Right Opinions That Are Held by All the Right People™. If we measure up, if we perform, then we're accepted. And if we don't, we belong in the outer darkness. No wonder we can be afraid that if we start talking more about Jesus, we won't be accepted.

Fear of Standing Out from the Crowd

The second fear is closely related to the first, and it concerns, once again, a common human desire: our urge to conform. I lived in

---

[2] My school specialised in soccer, cricket, and competitive folk music.

Canada for six years, and the Canadians had a term, originally borrowed from the Aussies, called "tall poppy syndrome." It refers to what often happens when somebody refuses to conform or, worse, dares to stick their head above the crowd. The imagery is pretty clear: when the farmer comes whistling by, trimming the hedgerow, the tall poppy doesn't get a sticker or a medal but a fairly brutal cutting down to size.[3]

We live in an increasingly conformist culture, and many of us are nervous about standing out from the crowd. Yet speaking up about Jesus at work or school means doing just that—we are immediately going to look different, like my six-foot-five friend who sent me a picture of himself standing in a crowded shopping mall in Indonesia, a country where the average height is five foot two. "See if you can spot the tourist," he had captioned the photo. Being a Christian in a sea of non-Christian friends or colleagues can feel just like that. And being a Christian who *talks* about their faith can feel like being not just a tall poppy but a sunflower in a field of tulips, waving at the farmer as he mows and shouting, "Hey, over here!"

Fear of Being Called Names

Another fear that holds many of us back is the fear of being called names or of being labelled with terrifying adjectives if we publicly identify as a Christian. As a child, I remember complaining to my teacher that some kid in class had called me a rude name. The teacher smiled sweetly and responded with the old proverb "Sticks and stones may break your bones, but words can never

---

[3] The Canadians even applied this philosophy on a national level. The year we moved to Canada, 2010, was also the year the Winter Olympics were held in Vancouver, and it was a cause of tremendous angst among parts of the Canadian media that their athletes had done *too* well (landing fourteen gold medals) and thus the country stood out way too dramatically in the medal table.

hurt you." Only that's not true, is it? Words can wound. And sometimes in the culture wars raging today, Christians can feel like we're being beaten about the head with the entire *Concise Oxford English Dictionary*,[4] so ready are people to tell us what they think of religion in general and Christianity in particular.

I remember a flight a few years after my fear of flying had been cured. Shortly after takeoff, I got talking to the passenger next to me. I found out all about him—why he was travelling from Toronto to Vancouver, his work, his family, and so on. After about fifteen minutes of chatting, he asked me, "So what do you do for a living?" I've learnt that saying cheerfully, "I'm a Christian evangelist" often leads to people running for the emergency exits or hiding under the seat, so I softballed it slightly. "I'm a Christian writer, speaker, and broadcaster," I replied. Instantly his whole demeanour changed. "I *hate* the church!" he snapped. "Christians are homophobic, transphobic, misogynistic, and irrational." And those were just the words I could spell.

In the eyes of many of our friends, neighbours, and colleagues, the issue is not so much that Christianity is *false* or *untrue* but that Christianity is *bad*—that Christians are horrible and oppressive people, especially because of what we think about sexuality, gender, or a range of other progressive causes. As my Australian friend Stephen McAlpine put it in his helpful book on the subject, we're no longer seen as the *good* guys; we're increasingly seen as the *bad* guys.[5] And therefore we worry that if we try to talk about Jesus to our friends, classmates, or colleagues, we'll get labelled with some horribly negative term.

---

[4] Which is admittedly less painful than being whacked with a thesaurus—for that can hurt, injure, impair, maim, wound, and incapacitate.

[5] See Stephen McAlpine, *Being the Bad Guys: How to Live for Jesus in a World That Says You Shouldn't* (Epsom, UK: Good Book Company, 2021).

Fear of Causing Arguments or Division

A fourth fear that consumes many of us is the worry that if we try to talk about our faith, it will result in arguments and disagreements. When it comes to the question of whether arguments are a good thing, let's be honest: Western culture can't entirely make up its mind. On the one hand, many of our social media spaces are quite literally fuelled by argument. On Twitter especially, things can get heated very quickly, and it can be fruitless trying to calm down the nuclear reaction of invective by inserting the control rods of logic and reason. Without arguments, I think the Internet would largely cease to exist, or at least fail to make the kind of profits needed to fuel Jeff Bezos's next trip to space. Yet on the other hand, in many real-world social settings, if a conversation looks like it's getting at all argumentative, people get nervous. We live in a deeply and increasingly divided society and so, we're told, we must *never*—at work, at the dinner table, at school—bring up topics like religion because that could divide people. Far better to pick topics that unite—like politics. (Or maybe not.)

Thus Christians, who naturally feel compelled by our faith in Christ to be conciliatory and compassionate, can particularly feel pressured here. No wonder we are often tempted to shy away from talking about our faith for fear that it will cause division or, if we're brave enough to try it on social media, result in our being doused in kerosene and torched by the mob. Better just to say nothing, right?

Fear of the Implications for My Career

A fifth fear that often underlies our nervousness is fear of the implications for our career should we speak up about Jesus. Let's be honest: many workplaces have become political minefields, where using an incorrect word or expressing the wrong idea can result in a ton of grief landing on you in the shape of the HR department. With so much of workplace (and campus) life viewed through the lens of harm and harm reduction, just think what could happen if you talked to your colleague, Arnold, about your faith in Jesus, he asked you what Christians believe about sexuality, and Arnold then complained to HR that your answer triggered him or made him feel unsafe. No wonder many Christians, terrified of the consequences of a conversation going wrong, simply self-censor at work or university.

Not that saying nothing necessarily saves you here. A friend of mine, James, who worked in the local branch of a large multinational company, ran into an issue whereby a directive came down from HR saying that the company planned to show its support for the LGBTQIA+ community by actively celebrating Pride Month. And to that end, every staff member was expected to stick the provided rainbow poster above their desk. What should a Christian like James do at this point? Push back hard and risk a disciplinary hearing or losing his job? Say nothing and conform whilst shrivelling inside with guilt? In the end, James thought of a brilliant solution: he went to the HR department, expressed how wonderful he thought it was that the company was concerned about justice issues, but then shared that he felt the LGBTQIA+ community already got a lot of attention. "On the other hand," James said, "I have long been a supporter of the Free Tibet movement and its campaign for liberty for the Tibetan people. If you don't mind, rather than put up a Pride poster, I'm going to stick a Free Tibet poster above my desk." There was no pushback (it probably wasn't a good look for the HR manager to say, "No, we don't mind the Tibetans being oppressed"), and so for the next fortnight, James found that his unique poster started all kinds of conversations, some even about faith—and he'd done it without stepping on any career-ending landmines.

Fear of Being Asked a Question I Can't Answer

A sixth common fear that can prevent us sharing our faith in Jesus more openly is the worry about what would happen if someone raised a question or objection to which we did not know the answer. It's worth asking yourself what that question might look like for you. What is the question about your faith that, if a colleague or friend asked you, would be so utterly, devastatingly, toe-curlingly terrifying, that it would be better if the ground opened up and swallowed you whole, rather than you having to address the Question of Doom? Maybe for you it's a question about sexuality, science, suffering, or sausages, or even a question beginning with a letter other than *s*.

The good news is there are several later chapters in this book specifically devoted to equipping you to engage with tough questions about your faith. But in the meantime, I wonder whether the fact that some of us are nervous about this issue is a gentle reminder that as Christians we can't escape the urgent need to ensure we are thinking through our beliefs. Nowhere does the Bible commend blind faith, and whilst it describes faith as a gift, nowhere does Scripture suggest it is the gift of stupidity. Maybe some of us need to take more seriously the exhortation in 1 Peter 3:15 to *be prepared* to give a reason for our hope.

At the same time, it can also be helpful to remember that just because you don't know the answer to the question doesn't mean there *isn't* an answer. There are many things I don't know. I don't know how gravity works. I don't know how many gallons of coffee are drunk by Swedes each year. I don't know why we never seem to see baby pigeons. But just because *I* don't know doesn't mean *nobody* knows. Similarly, over the years it has been a huge encouragement to me that in God's family there are many brilliant men and women whose brains are considerably bigger than mine and who are utterly convinced that Christianity is true. We are surrounded by a great cloud of witnesses, and if we're sometimes afraid of tough questions, that can be an encouraging thought.

Fear of Failure

The first six fears we have considered concern how others—our friends, colleagues, and neighbours—might respond to us if we try to talk to them about Jesus. Those are some of the most common fears that hold us back. But there are also two *spiritual* fears that for some of us can be equally crippling—and the first is fear of failure.

What happens, we wonder, *if I pluck up the courage to share my faith with a friend and, although the conversation goes well (I don't get fired, ostracised, or have coconuts or sharks thrown at me), they don't respond?* Perhaps you have had that very experience: you have talked about Jesus with a friend or colleague—maybe you've had many conversations with somebody over the years—and yet they still seem far from faith.

Of all the wily tricks the devil would play on us to keep us from talking about Jesus with joy and vigour, this is one of the sneakiest: whispering quietly into our ears the lie that making someone believe is *our* job. That if we're clever enough, articulate enough, or holy enough, or our teeth are perfect enough, then we can win people for Jesus through the sheer force of our efforts. As the lie takes hold, we take onto our shoulders the responsibility for our friend's spiritual state, and it's a load too heavy to bear. We groan beneath the weight, the spring goes from our step, and if they don't respond, we blame ourselves, concluding that there must be something wrong with us, that we're a failure, and that maybe our spiritual gift is stacking the cakes or serving the chairs after church meetings, rather than talking to people about Jesus.

So let's remember that salvation is ultimately God's job. It is God who calls people, whose Spirit works to soften their hearts and convict them of sin. It is Jesus whose beauty, love, and grace will draw people to him. We have the privilege—and the calling—to be faithful witnesses as best we can but to do so knowing and trusting that whether we are amazing at telling others about Jesus or terrible (remember Jonah!), God is the one who will work through us when and where he chooses. The more you let that realisation sink in, the more it will take the pressure off and release you to share Jesus naturally. Incidentally, that realisation will also make you less likely to come across like a secondhand car salesperson who is working on commission or like a cunning chess player who just wants to win.

Fear of Making God Look Bad

And so we come to the last of our eight fears—and it's one that hadn't occurred to me until I was talking to a Christian student one day who startled me by announcing, "I'm so rubbish at evangelism that the best thing I can do for Jesus is say absolutely nothing. I'd probably do more harm than good if I tried to talk to my friends about Jesus, so I'm just going to keep quiet." And maybe you can identify with that student. Perhaps even right now you're humming alternate words to that classic Christian hymn: "Shut up, shut up for Jesus . . ."

This particular fear doesn't always express itself so directly. Sometimes it can come out more subtly. Back in my Undercover Christian days, I recall thinking that even though I wasn't *talking* about Jesus at work, I could nevertheless *live* for Jesus at work. If I tried hard to be a model friend and perfect colleague, if I was terribly nice and served my colleagues well—if I washed up everybody else's coffee mugs, mentored younger staff members, or volunteered to run the interdepartmental Extreme Snakes and Ladders league—then somehow my behaviour would draw people to Jesus. My *words* might be so clumsy they could bring the gospel into disrepute, but maybe my *actions* would speak louder. Of course, the problem here is that whilst we're certainly called to live Christlike lives, if that's *all* we do, the likelihood is our colleagues won't automatically connect this to Jesus. Rather, they'll just assume we're nice people, and thus there's an irony that trying to live for Jesus without *any* words can end up drawing the attention not to Jesus but to ourselves. And another challenging question: Are we being good colleagues because we think it's a brilliant pointer to Jesus or simply because we want people to like us?

Fear Reveals Our Idols

I hope you have found looking at some of the common fears that hold us back from sharing our faith to be helpful. Not least, it can be encouraging to know you're not alone in experiencing them. For, another of the insidious wiles of the devil is to isolate us, to make us think that every other Christian is brilliant at telling others about Jesus whilst it's only we who are the spiritual equivalent of Shaggy from *Scooby-Doo*, hiding knock-kneed behind the sofa in terror.

Speaking of *Scooby-Doo*, almost every episode of that classic cartoon series ends with the literal unmasking of the ghost or beastie that's been terrorising people, revealing that it wasn't really some frightful monster but just an ordinary human being wearing a costume. And in the same way, naming and identifying our fears about evangelism can unmask them, perhaps revealing them as not quite so terrifying as we at first thought.

Poking fun at them helps too. In the early days of our marriage, when money was tight, my wife would sometimes encourage me to name the things I was afraid of because of our finances (losing our home, being forced to sleep on a park bench, and having to get a second job as a taxidermist) and then to laugh at the ridiculousness of the fear in question. Indeed, we can sometimes miss that one of the joys of the gospel is that it enables us to laugh in the face of fear, even the fear of death. In 1925, the playwright Eugene O'Neill wrote *Lazarus Laughed*, a play that explores this idea. Think about it: How could you scare Lazarus after Jesus had raised him from the dead? What could you threaten Lazarus with? The play ends with a frustrated Roman Emperor Tiberius sentencing Lazarus to death, yet even as the sentence is passed, Lazarus laughs—for what Jesus has shown him and done for him has made all fears look ridiculous.

But there's one last reason why taking a careful look at our fears can be helpful: because our fears can reveal where our idols lie, where our identity is located, and what our hearts most deeply desire. If you fear losing your job, then your idol may be security. If you fear failing an exam, your idol may be Performance Based Acceptance. If you fear getting outbid on eBay for that novelty lava lamp in the shape of Big Bird from *Sesame Street*—well, maybe you just need help.

But if our fears reveal our idols, could the same be true when it comes to some of our fears about sharing our faith? Could it just be that perhaps we are at risk of making an idol out of our desire for a comfortable, easy life—and that against that background, telling others about Jesus looks a bit too risky? That possibility has, oddly enough, been recognised by some atheists.

One of my favourite entertainers is Penn Jillette, one half of the world-famous comedy magic double-act Penn and Teller. His live shows and TV series have been watched by millions. He's also an outspoken atheist, well-known for his blistering attacks on Christianity. But a few years ago, he surprised his fans by releasing a video blog called "A Gift of a Bible."[6] In the video, Jillette tells the story of a man who came up to him following a show and, after complimenting him on his performance, nervously presented him with the gift of a Bible, saying, "I wanted you to have this." Jillette remarked what courage this must have taken, given his reputation as a fiery atheist. But then, rather than criticising the man for his religious faith, Jillette continued,

> I don't respect people who don't proselytize. I don't respect that at all. If you believe that there's a heaven and hell and people could be going to hell or not getting eternal life or whatever, and you think that, well, it's not really worth telling them this because it would make it socially awkward! . . . How much do you have to hate somebody to not proselytize? How much do you have to hate somebody to believe that everlasting life is possible and not tell them that? I mean, if I believed beyond a

---

6 The video is available on YouTube. Penn Jillette (reposted by beinzee), "A Gift of a Bible," July 8, 2010, YouTube video, 5:11, https://youtu.be/6md638smQd8.

shadow of a doubt that a truck was coming at you and you didn't believe it, but that truck was bearing down on you, there's a certain point where I tackle you. And this is more important than that.

Penn Jillette is absolutely right. If we truly believe the message of the gospel, that a person's eternal destiny depends on them hearing and responding to the incredible news about Jesus, how can we possibly conceive of keeping this to ourselves? Yes, it may be scary (although it's not likely you'll ever have to approach a loudmouthed celebrity atheist like Penn Jillette), but if we *really* believe the gospel, if we *really* believe that without Jesus our friends are facing an eternity without God, surely it's worth a few risks to share that news with them.

Our Reaction to Fear

Almost all Christians experience a degree of fear when it comes to sharing our faith in Jesus, and doing so doesn't make us second-class Christians. But what is crucial is how we respond to our fears. Scientists tell us that human beings have two deeply wired circuits in our brain when it comes to fear: fight or flight. This has nothing to do with the agonizing choice over whether to watch *Rocky* or *Airplane!* when we're in the mood for a classic movie but concerns our tendency, when faced with fear, to become fierce, confrontational, and confident—or to turn tail and run.

Interestingly, the fight-or-flight reaction sometimes kicks in for Christians when we're faced with an increasingly mad culture, one which seems to be driving from Post-Christian-Ville to Outright-Bonkers-Burg faster every day. Some Christians feel the need to scream and shout at the culture, hoping that sheer volume might do what expository sermons haven't.[7] Other Christians respond to the culture by running away and hiding or musing about building monasteries in the back garden and withdrawing from society completely.

And the same polarised reactions can sometimes manifest themselves when we think about sharing our faith. We can think we have to become (or worse, suffer the delusion that we already are) the world's *boldest* evangelist, or we screw ourselves up with guilt and imagine we're the world's *worst* evangelist. In his marvellous little book *The Screwtape Letters*, C. S. Lewis imagines a correspondence between a senior and a junior devil, the former advising the latter how best to torment and trip up his "patient." In one letter, the experienced and wily tempter, Screwtape, touches on this very theme. He advises Wormwood, his young charge, to try to get the Christian he is tempting to either boldly overestimate his abilities or tie himself up in knots at his inadequacy. Screwtape writes, "Tortured fear and stupid confidence are both desirable states of mind."[8]

Chances are, if you were prone to stupid confidence, you wouldn't be reading this book. So given that some variety of "tortured fear" is more likely your temptation, take heart: most Christians have, at some point or other, faced most of the fears in this chapter (and others) when it comes to evangelism. Fear is totally normal. But it's not where we want to remain. "Do not fear" is the Bible's frequent advice to us. So how *do* we move beyond fear? That's what we'll begin to explore in the next chapter.

---

[7] A Canadian friend of mine said he used to enjoy listening to *really* shouty preachers, as it made him feel motivated, until his wife calmly asked him one day, "Sweetie, would you buy a refrigerator from a man who extolled its merits in *that* tone of voice?"

[8] C. S. Lewis, *The Screwtape Letters* (London: William Collins, 2016), 75.

CHAPTER 3

THE FIRST STEPS TO FEAR-LESS EVANGELISM

I ONCE WORKED FOR A BOSS WHO HAD a thing for motivational posters. As a team, we could be a dour bunch, but our fearless leader was utterly convinced that if she hung enough inspirational quotes around the office, it would exponentially improve productivity, morale, and team spirit. Thus, we would find, hanging on the walls, beautiful landscape photographs accompanied by sayings like "All things are difficult before they are easy," "Team: Together Everyone Achieves More," and (above the office first-aid station, as I recall) "Mistakes are simply proof that you're trying."

This attempt to motivate the staff toward success came to a somewhat bitter end when one of my more sarcastically inclined colleagues discovered the website Despair.com, which specialises in parodying the entire motivational industry. A secret whip-round was organised and some *de*motivational posters purchased, and I will never forget the staff meeting, a few days later, at which the regional manager was in attendance. Mid presentation, he looked up to see, hanging on the walls of the board room, slogans that included "Meetings: None of Us Is as Dumb as All of Us," "Achievement: You Can Do Anything You Set Your Mind to When You Have Vision, Determination, and an Endless Supply of Expendable Labour," and my personal favourite, "Eagles May Soar, but Weasels Don't Get Sucked into Jet Engines." Nothing was ever said, but from that day forth, never was a motivational poster seen again on the office walls.

The simple fact is that platitudes don't change attitudes. You cannot shift people's behaviour with simplistic catchphrases, nor can you change your own behaviour just with gritted teeth and sheer willpower. You only need to glance at the near-infinite number of New Year's resolutions shipwrecked on the rocks of reality come February 1 to realise that it takes more than a few words to change deeply ingrained habits.

And the same is true when it comes to evangelism, especially overcoming the fear, reluctance, and nervousness that can hold us back from sharing our faith in Jesus with our friends, neighbours, and colleagues. It's going to require more than soundbites, the occasional inspirational sermon, or the youth pastor trying to persuade the youth group with the sheer force of his personality that *Street Evangelism Will Be Fun, Really!*

Good luck with that.

But even worse than trying to *enthuse* people into sharing their faith is trying to *guilt* them into it, perhaps by directly or indirectly implying that they're second-rate Christians or are somehow letting the side down by not sharing their faith more proactively. The problem with that approach is that it simply plays into the fear-guilt cycle that so easily builds up around evangelism. We don't share our faith confidently and easily because we're afraid (perhaps for some of the reasons discussed in the last chapter). This makes us feel guilty and generally negative—which makes us far more prone to fear. And thus the loop repeats, faster and faster, like a washing machine on a spin cycle, whilst our confidence gurgles away down the drain.

By my midtwenties, I had sat through dozens of sermons, bought talks by famous Christian speakers on CD,[1] and read books with titles like *Evangelism for Dummies* and *Proselytism for Prats*, most of which tried enthusiasm or guilt-tripping, and none of them helped. None really addressed the basic fears that had caused me to become an Undercover Christian. At most they occasionally motivated me to pray a bit more fervently about sharing my faith, but not really to *try* it. Just as the young St. Augustine famously prayed in his preconversion days, "Lord, make me chaste—but not yet," I found myself praying, at least subconsciously, "Lord, please open opportunities for me to share my faith. But please not today. And certainly not in my workplace!"

Then one day, as I was clearing out some old shelves, I came across a book I hadn't seen for years, one of my favourite stories from childhood—*Danny, the Champion of the World*, by British children's writer Roald Dahl.[2] It tells the story of the close relationship between eight-year-old Danny and his father (Danny's mother had died when he was a baby) and in particular how his father shares his love of pheasant poaching with his son. As a child I loved the story, even though there were no pheasants where we lived in London, and none of the poaching tricks that Danny learnt

---

[1] For younger readers, a CD is an MP3 that you can also use as a Frisbee or coffee coaster.

[2] Dahl is perhaps most famous for stories like *Charlie and the Chocolate Factory* and his lesser known book on the problems with long sermons, *James and the Giant Preach*.

worked on our local pigeon population (not, it must be said, for want of trying). But as I was flicking through the old book, I came across a line that leapt out at me. At one point, Danny makes the observation, "Most of the really exciting things we do in our lives scare us to death. They wouldn't be exciting if they didn't."[3]

When you stop and consider that for a moment, it's blindingly obvious. Whether it's trying out a new roller coaster at the theme park, or skydiving, or asking somebody to marry us, or making our first trip into the big city on our own—life is full of experiences that are not merely exciting *and* scary; rather, part of the reason they're exciting is *because* they're scary. But the scariness doesn't usually stop us because we know it's worth it for the thrill factor or the satisfaction of what we experience or accomplish.

The more I thought about Dahl's line, the more convinced I became that there was something in it. After all, one of my own occasional hobbies is rock climbing. I love the sense of achievement that comes with scaling a rock face or getting to the top of the climbing wall. Yet despite the enjoyment, I still find aspects of rock climbing pretty fear-inducing, especially abseiling. I've few problems going *up*, but when you get to the top and then have to lean back over the yawning precipice and rappel down to the bottom—well, that's never become any less scary, no matter how many times I've done it. It still feels a little like thumbing one's nose at gravity whilst hoping that gravity doesn't suddenly notice and take offence.

But despite all that, I still go climbing occasionally. I haven't swapped the vertical sport of rock climbing for something safer and more horizontal, such as curling or cheese-making. And why

---

3 Roald Dahl, *Danny, the Champion of the World* (London: Puffin, 2016), 54.

not? Well, first, because I love the excitement and the adrenaline rush of climbing and of exposed places: hanging off a cliff is a cheaper way to get the heart racing than a grande quad nonfat cappuccino at the local overpriced coffee shop. Second, because I've had a little training—I know how to don a harness, how to use the ropes, and how to ensure that rock climbing doesn't become skydiving for an exciting (if brief) moment. And, third, because I trust the person on the other end of the rope. The fact that at the end of the rope, keeping me safe, is a trusted friend or climbing instructor gives me confidence that even if things get a little scary, there's somebody I can rely on—and in the case of abseiling, somebody is quite literally holding my weight as I lean back. This means that even though my heart may be racing, I'm still going to do the climb.

My kids are now getting into the sport—going to the climbing wall is one of the highlights of our annual holidays in the English Lake District—and it's fun watching them learn exactly the same lessons. The initial terror ("You want me to climb up *there*, Dad?") slowly becomes enjoyment once they have had enough basic training to know what to do, developed a confidence that Dad won't let go of the rope (not even to take a sip of his grande quad nonfat cappuccino), and realised that the fun and sense of achievement that comes from climbing makes the scariness something worth experiencing. Shouting "Fear is for wimps! Get up that rock face!" is never going to work. But excitement, confidence, and trust can.

And then one day it suddenly occurred to me that all the same things are true of evangelism. If we truly believe the gospel—if we reflect on who Jesus is, what he has done in our lives, and why it is we *want* to share him with others—surely that's incredibly exciting, right? Likewise, when we hear testimonies or read stories of people coming to faith in Christ, it gets us excited. That's why books of dramatic conversion stories, with titles like *From Murder to Methodism: How a Granny-Murdering Psychopath Found Jesus*, sell so well. But as we've seen, excitement and scariness often go together. We shouldn't therefore be surprised that evangelism is at times a bit scary—exciting things usually are.

By the way, I'm also a big believer in the idea that words really matter, so I think it can be helpful to tease out an important difference between two words that are all too often used interchangeably—namely, *scary* and *fear*. The word *scary* is best used to describe the *thing* in question: the dinosaur, the dentist, the climbing wall, and the prospect of sharing our faith can be *scary*. On the other hand, the word *fear* describes our emotional *response* to the scary thing: "I saw the giant man-eating dentist, and I was, like, totally *afraid*." Why it's important to separate the two ideas is that there's nothing particularly wrong with finding something scary. Looking over the fifty-foot vertical drop you're about to abseil down and thinking, *Whoa, that's scary!* doesn't mean anything more than that you've got good eyesight, you aren't stupid, and your self-preservation circuits are wired correctly. And as we've seen, scariness and excitement tend to go together. By contrast, the problem with fear is that if we're not careful, it can root us to the ground and freeze us, and that's not helpful, either when we should be escaping from the dinosaur or when we get stuck in sharing our faith. It's noteworthy that the Bible has lots of encouragements, exhortations, and warnings not to fear, but it doesn't chastise us for finding things scary.

However, separating out scariness from fear and recognising that excitement and scariness go together isn't enough when it comes to sharing our faith. Rather, we need to consider two other factors from our rock-climbing example. First, the importance of basic training—some simple tools that can help us—so we're not engaged in the evangelistic equivalent of leaping off the top of the cliff shouting, "Geronimo!" or trying to climb the north face of the Eiger using suckers on our boots. And second, the crucial need to have confidence in the person holding the end of the rope, which reminds us that we are not called to do evangelism unsupported but rather in the knowledge and trust that we're being held up and carried.

In 1 Peter 3:14-16 (a passage we briefly touched on in the last chapter), Peter—a man who had learnt by this point in his life a few lessons about rushing in or making rash assumptions about his abilities—wrote these words:

> Do not fear what they fear; do not be frightened. But in your hearts set apart Christ as Lord. Always be prepared to give an answer to everyone who asks you to give the reason for the hope that you have. But do this with gentleness and respect, keeping a clear conscience, so that those who speak maliciously against your good behaviour in Christ may be ashamed of their slander.

Notice that Peter is very honest about the temptation we have toward fear. Indeed, he mentions fear three times in this passage, not least because he's writing to an audience who had every reason to be afraid. At the time when Peter wrote this letter, the first waves of Roman persecution against Christians had begun. One of the worst bullies, the emperor Nero, was notorious for his viciousness. Among his favourite party pieces was to tie Christians to stakes in his palace gardens, cover them in tar, then set them alight to entertain his guests. We are worried we might lose our jobs for sharing our faith; the Christians to whom Peter is writing might literally be *fired* by Nero for refusing to denounce Christ.

But despite that pretty scary context, Peter doesn't write advice like "Keep your heads down until Nero has died" or "Secretly leave Christian tracts under the windscreen wipers of cars in the parking lot at the Colosseum."[4] Rather, Peter offers his readers some very practical suggestions. First, keep focussed on Christ—revere him as Lord (remember that he's got the end of the rope!). Second, be prepared (maybe learn some practical tools for sharing your faith with your neighbours). And third, don't forget to do all this in such a way that people are struck by your gentleness and respect as you talk about your hope in Jesus. And if you know anything about church history, you'll remember what happened as the first Christians put this into practice: the church grew from 120 people in AD 33 to over 31 million in AD 350. Or to put it another way, from 0 percent of the Roman Empire to 52.9 percent in roughly 300 years.[5]

"It's Too Risky!"

I appreciate that all of this may still sound considerably counter-intuitive, not least because we live in such a risk-averse age. For many decades now, Western culture has been operating on the basic maxim "If we can remove even the slightest prospect of risk, we ought to." Sometimes this risk-averseness hits insane levels of daftness, such as the town near us whose politicians arranged for all the low branches on every tree on town property to be sawn

---

4 I know what you're thinking: that's an anachronism. The Colosseum wasn't built until *after* Nero's death.
5 Those figures are drawn from Rodney Stark, *The Triumph of Christianity: How the Jesus Movement Became the World's Largest Religion* (New York: HarperOne, 2011), 157.

off (because kids might climb the trees and get hurt), or airlines putting "Danger: May Contain Nuts" warnings on packets of in-flight peanuts.

The same risk-averseness can affect how we think about shar-ing our faith, whether it's our own need to talk about Jesus with our friends or even how we think about the stories of missionaries from the past. For example, when we read those famous words of Jim Elliot, the American missionary martyred by Waodani tribes-people in Ecuador—"He is no fool who gives what he cannot keep to gain that which he cannot lose"—I wonder whether our instinctive reaction is to say, "Amen!" or to think, *Dude, you were a bit extreme.* The idea of taking evangelism so far that it might cost one's life is, I suspect, increasingly alien to a Western church that at times looks as risk averse as the culture.

Given all that I said earlier in this chapter about cheesy moti-vational quotes, posters, and sermons, most of which are about as effective as a rubber pickaxe, I realise I can't deconstruct our tendency to lean towards risk-aversion with a soundbite. But we can at least be aware of the way our culture infects us in this area, we can pray for the Lord's help for our minds and hearts to be shaped by a more biblical view, and perhaps we can think about a few small baby steps of risk we might take in sharing our faith.

The Way Ahead
All of which helpfully gives us a road map for the rest of the book. In the next chapter, we're going to look at some examples of people sharing their faith at work, at university, or among their friends and see if we can notice some common threads in what they're doing. Drawing from those examples, I'll introduce you to some

simple tools that can help you become at least 64.3 percent more confident[6] in talking about Jesus with your friends and family, neighbours and colleagues. And as we do all of that, we'll keep in mind who is, as it were, on the other end of the rope. Evangelism isn't ultimately about learning the right tools or techniques, clever presentations, or witty one-liners, or about offering the right dessert at the church bring-and-share supper. It is ultimately *God's* task—we get the privilege of working with him as he draws people to himself. Primarily what God asks of us is not our capability but our availability.

One final thought. Throughout this chapter, I've used the analogy of rock climbing, mainly because it's a sport I'm familiar with. But the one weakness of rock climbing is it's mostly a solo sport, like archery or jogging.[7] But the majority of sports are *team* sports. To succeed at football or cricket[8] or basketball requires not one or two gifted individuals but for the entire team to play well *as a team*. And the same is true when it comes to evangelism: we have varying strengths and styles. God has wired each of us in different ways, and we will reach others most effectively when we learn to play well to our strengths and lean on others in places where we are weak. Peter makes this very point a chapter further on from where we were just reading. He writes,

> Each of you should use whatever gift you have received
> to serve others, as faithful stewards of God's grace in its
> various forms. If anyone speaks, they should do so as one
> who speaks the very words of God. If anyone serves, they

---

6 Remember that 47.3 percent of statistics are simply made up on the spot.

7 The Bible is not in favour of jogging, warning in Proverbs 28:1, "Only the wicked run when nobody is pursuing them."

8 For American readers, cricket is like baseball, only with history, culture, and regular breaks for afternoon tea.

should do so with the strength God provides, so that in all things God may be praised through Jesus Christ.

I PETER 4:10-11

Thinking about evangelism as a team sport also reminds us of the need to encourage one another so that nobody feels their task is to do evangelism as some kind of Lone Ranger, out in the Badlands battling the challenges of sharing Jesus entirely on their own. In the late 1990s, when I began to engage Muslims in conversations at Speakers' Corner in London,[9] one of the things that kept me coming back, despite the difficulty and nervousness it involved, was that I wasn't doing it alone. There was a team of twenty of us who headed out each Sunday afternoon from All Souls Church in London, spent two hours in conversation with others about Jesus, then sat down over a fast-food supper and debriefed. We shared stories of what had gone well and what had gone badly, and we encouraged one another, laughed together, cried together, and prayed together. That sense of comradery, the encouragement of being supported, of not being alone in evangelism, made it so much easier to face the fears of sharing my faith. So whether you're wanting to share your faith at work, among friends, or at university, make sure you have other Christians whom you can ask to pray for you while you're doing it, with whom you can share stories afterwards of how it went, and who can commiserate or rejoice with you whatever happens.

Finally, the other advantage of thinking about evangelism as a team sport is that it reminds you that you can learn from others who have been playing the game for longer than you have. There

---

9 I tell this story in Andy Bannister, *Do Muslims and Christians Worship the Same God?* (London: InterVarsity Press, 2021), 6–13.

is, as they say, nothing new under the sun.[10] So in the next chapter, we'll look at some stories of Christians sharing their faith naturally with their friends, neighbours, and colleagues and see if there's anything we can learn. And I promise you, there won't be a simplistic motivational quote in sight.

---

10 Especially where I live, given that the British climate has so little of it.

CHAPTER 4

EVANGELISM
IN EVERYDAY PLACES

LET'S BE HONEST, there is at times something of a celebrity culture in the church. We do so love our Christian superstars. There are the famous preachers, whose videos have been watched by millions and whose books have sold by the wagonload.[1] Then there are the celebrity worship leaders whose songs we love to sing along to (often tunelessly, in my family's case) in the car, kitchen, bath, or sometimes even in church.

In yet another league are the celebrity testimonies. Whether it's a film or sports star who has turned to Christ or a former gangster who wows audiences with tales of how he used to smoke grannies and murder drugs before Jesus rescued him, we love stories of famous repentant sinners.

---

[1] I find it hard to even get my head around a sales figure like the fifty million copies of Rick Warren's guide to Christianity for dolphins, *The Porpoise Driven Life*.

There is nothing *inherently* wrong with celebrity preachers or worship leaders or those with dramatic testimonies. We are grateful to God for them, for their lives have had an impact on many, and they often grapple with pressures of fame that we can scarcely imagine. Who of us, for example, would want Joel Osteen's dentistry bill?

But at the same time that celebrity Christians inspire us, sometimes their stories can also be deeply disempowering. And this is particularly true when it comes to celebrity evangelists, the kind of people who can fill stadiums to overflowing or whose book *How I Brought the Entirety of My City to Christ before Breakfast* made the *New York Times* Best Sellers list. Sometimes the more gifted the evangelist, the more they actually demotivate us rather than inspire us, as we look at them and think, *I couldn't possibly do what they're doing.*

I first had my eyes opened to this when we lived in Canada. The organisation for which I worked had arranged to bring Professor John Lennox, one of the most brilliant and articulate Christians when it comes to questions around faith and science, over from the UK for a speaking tour. John spoke at several Canadian universities as well as at a large church in Toronto, where 2,500 people turned up to hear him. It was a brilliant event, and I was thrilled how Canadians had responded to John. But then a colleague brought me down to earth with a bump.

"Have you seen some of the feedback from the church event with John?" my colleague, Rick, asked. I replied that I had not, so he read out some of the responses to a survey we had emailed to attendees. Response after response ran along these lines: "Loved the event. Loved John. Grateful to God for him because there is no way I could do what he does."

Rick looked at me thoughtfully. "Is that *good* feedback?" he asked. "Is it actually our goal to have people go away thinking they can't do evangelism, and besides, they don't *need* to do evangelism because God has sent somebody massively more brilliant than them who can?"

Empowerment Beats Inspiration

We get inspired by big, famous names and the skills they can demonstrate. But in terms of empowerment—of feeling equipped to actually do something *ourselves*—that is often far better accomplished when, rather than celebrities or experts, we see people who are just like us.

In the previous chapter, I used the example of rock climbing, a sport I have messed around with over the years. I love watching films about it, of which my favourite in recent years is probably *Free Solo*. The movie tells the story of Alex Honnold, one of the best climbers for a generation, and his ascent—entirely unroped—of El Capitan in Yosemite National Park, among the hardest rock faces in the world. Watching Honnold scamper up vertiginous granite cliffs like Spiderman's second cousin is awe-inspiring, and I've rewatched the movie many times. But my reaction every time is not "I must go to the climbing wall tomorrow; it's been months!" but "There's no way I could do that! Pass the popcorn." Conversely, imagine if I do make it to the climbing wall at the crack of dawn one Saturday morning, dragged there by one of my offspring who has yet to discover the meaning of the words *lethargy, procrastination,* or indeed, *lie in.* If there at the climbing wall I see a few guys just like me—in their late forties, mildly unfit, and packing a few extra pounds—managing to get up the wall, then I'm far more tempted to think, *If that dude can do it . . .*

When it comes to evangelism (and to Christian discipleship in general), the same thing applies. We may be *inspired* by those who are famous, but we are far more likely to be *empowered* by those who are just like us.[2] Scripture makes this point, too, perhaps most famously in 1 Corinthians 12, where the apostle Paul compares the church to a body. Just as a body is made up of many different parts, some more glamourous and showy than others, nevertheless each part is vital—and above all, no part should ever think it is too insignificant to be of any use:

> The body is not made up of one part but of many. Now if the foot should say, "Because I am not a hand, I do not belong to the body," it would not for that reason stop being part of the body. And if the ear should say, "Because I am not an eye, I do not belong to the body," it would not for that reason stop being part of the body. If the whole body were an eye, where would the sense of hearing be? If the whole body were an ear, where would the sense of smell be? But in fact God has placed the parts in the body, every one of them, just as he wanted them to be. If they were all one part, where would the body be? As it is, there are many parts, but one body.
>
> The eye cannot say to the hand, "I don't need you!" And the head cannot say to the feet, "I don't need you!" On the contrary, those parts of the body that seem to be weaker are indispensable, and the parts that we think are less honourable we treat with special honour. . . . so that

---

[2] This was our thinking at Solas behind the *Frontlines* series, where we interviewed dozens of Christians in different types of jobs about how they lived out and shared their faith in the workplace. The feedback we received showed how much people value learning from those who are just like them. Check out the series at http://www.solas-cpc .org/frontlines/.

there should be no division in the body, but that its parts should have equal concern for each other.

I CORINTHIANS 12:14-23, 25

When it comes to evangelism, we need those who can reach thousands at a time, the power of their words or their stories pointing people to Christ. But just as eyes and ears are important to the body, it also needs many, many more ordinary parts. We have two eyes but ten feet of small intestine, 213 bones, and trillions upon trillions of mitochondria. And as a friend once put it, "Maybe we don't need another million-dollar evangelist; maybe we need a million one-dollar evangelists." So be encouraged, because we all have a role to play. And the way to see that—and to learn how to play that role more effectively—may be to look away from the Christian celebrities and learn instead from those who are more like you.

As I look back over my own journey from fearfulness and playing at Undercover Christian to being more confident and willing to talk about my faith in Jesus, I realise how much I was helped along the way by ordinary Christians, friends in many cases, who were getting on with the task of sharing their faith in Jesus in everyday, ordinary ways—at school, at work, at the pub, and among their friends. People whose lives I could look at and think, *They're out there doing it, God is working through them, so maybe I can do this too.* Let me share with you a few of their stories.

"Too Normal for Church"

My friend Sarah had for years struggled with confidence when it came to sharing her faith, but then she began to notice that she had no trouble starting conversations with people she was already naturally interested in talking to: the girl behind the counter with the amazing pink hair, the man in the coffee shop queue wearing a T-shirt with a clever slogan. So her evangelistic strategy is to look for natural opportunities to take an interest in people, and in return they will often take an interest in her.

Sarah once told me a story about a coffee shop she'd dived into on the way to church one Sunday. Whilst waiting for the coffee to brew, she'd begun chatting happily to the woman behind the counter, who had then said to her, "You look very nice. Where are you off to all dressed up this morning?"

Sarah cheerfully replied, "I'm off to church!"

The barista laughed and said, "Yeah, very funny! Where are you *really* going?"

"No, really," Sarah had replied, "I'm going to church. Why do you find that so odd?"

The barista thought for a moment and replied, "Well . . . you look too normal to go to church!" That gave Sarah a great opportunity to gently explain how lots of younger people go to church and to have an open, natural conversation about why she loved church because she loved Jesus—and church was an opportunity to spend time with others who loved him too.

Planting a Faith Flag

Finding opportunities to talk about church is actually one of the most natural ways to *begin* talking about our faith with our friends, yet sometimes we shy away from even mentioning it. I was chatting recently with a Christian nurse, Georgie, who early in her career discovered the importance—and the relative ease—of, as she puts it, "flying a faith flag at work." When the what-did-you-do-on-the-weekend conversation comes up on Monday morning,

Georgie has learnt that rather than just talk about everything she did on Saturday, if she plucks up the courage to include in her list of weekend activities a little faith flag like "and I went to a brilliant church service on Sunday," that can start a surprising number of conversations. If Georgie meets a new person from a town where she knows a church, she'll find the chance to say something like "I don't know Little Dribbling on the Marsh that well,[3] but I remember going to a church service there a few years ago." Regularly flying these kinds of faith flags over the years has led to deeper conversations about Jesus, when people have sometimes said things like "You're a Christian—what do you think about . . . ?" Georgie's aim is to get people asking *her* questions, rather than feeling the need to force every conversation toward her faith, which might scare colleagues off.

Befriending Buddhists

Being wise in conversations and not scaring people off is something that Sarah, whom we met earlier, has also been careful about in her friendships. Over the years, Sarah has befriended many people from different faith backgrounds, especially Buddhists, and quickly discovered that saying things like "You need to leave Buddhism immediately and follow Jesus" destroys both the hope of any further conversations and the friendship. But Sarah has discovered that she *can* say things to a Buddhist friend like this: "Do you mind if I ask you a question? Could we take a look together at the question of suffering? I would love to know what you think and believe about this, and then I'd love to share what I think Jesus has to say about the topic." That approach has led to many fruitful

---

[3] Before American readers snort in disdain at the daft things we Brits name our towns and villages, let me simply say "Bugtussle, Kentucky" and "Intercourse, Pennsylvania" and leave it at that.

conversations, and Sarah has friends who are now slowly walking towards Jesus. But it's been crucial that her friends have been able to see that Sarah genuinely values their opinions and is willing to ask questions and listen, not just preach at them.

Taxi Talk

Another friend of mine, Nigel, is an ex-military man who, despite the confidence that often goes with a military career, still sometimes finds it hard to get into conversations about Jesus. Nevertheless, Nigel has developed a knack for engaging naturally with the people the Lord brings across his path. On one occasion Nigel had been attending a weeklong Christian conference but had to leave the event midweek to play in a tennis tournament for two days. A taxi came to drive him to the railway station, and after exchanging pleasantries, Bill the taxi driver asked Nigel, "So what's the event going on at the conference centre this week?" Nigel replied that it was a Christian conference, to which Bill immediately snapped, "Oh, you're not one of those religious types, are you?"

"What do you mean by that?" Nigel asked, and Bill launched into a tirade about all the things he hated about religion, especially the hypocrisy and the moralism. Nigel quietly prayed, wondering how on earth to respond to this barrage of criticism.

When Bill finally paused for breath, Nigel responded with a question he felt the Lord had brought to his mind: "Bill, have you ever heard of a man called Jesus?"

Somewhat wrong-footed by this, Bill replied that of course he had. Nigel said, "It occurs to me that the stuff you're talking about—all the bad things religion has done—that Jesus might agree with you. After all, Jesus reserved his fiercest words for the religious leaders of the day." That led to a much more open conversation, and when, two days later, Bill returned to drive Nigel back from the station to the conference, it had broken the ice enough for Nigel to give Bill a tract as they parted, which Bill said he would consider reading.

Fishing with Richard Dawkins

Breaking the ice and starting conversations is often the thing we struggle the most with when it comes to talking about Jesus with our friends, so over the years I've always been keen to learn from those who have found ways to do this naturally. One of the most intriguing examples I have ever come across is my friend James, who told me he had discovered an unusual way of starting spiritual conversations at the coffee shop where he worked. "Do you sing classic hymns while brewing cappuccinos?" I asked. "No, I'm a barista, not a baritone . . . but what I do is I go fishing with Richard Dawkins."

For those who are unfamiliar with the name, Dawkins is one of the world's most famous atheists, whose books on atheism have sold millions of copies.[4] "What," I wondered out loud, "is the notorious sceptic doing in your coffee shop—and how are you managing to go fishing together?"

"Aha," said James, delighted he'd intrigued and baffled me. "What I do is this. On my lunch break, I'll sit at a free table with one of Dawkins's books, cover upwards, next to me. It usually isn't long before somebody passing, or another staff member, catches sight of the book and says words to the effect of 'Good book, that!' To which I reply with something like 'Really? What did you find interesting about it?' or 'He writes well, but I've got a few

---

4 Dawkins's book on performing magic tricks with fish, *The Cod Illusion*, has not sold nearly so well.

questions about it—do you have a moment?'" James added, "You wouldn't believe how many conversations about faith I have managed to start by openly reading books on atheism!"[5]

Books and Belief

Using books as a way to start conversations about faith is an idea that two Canadian friends of mine, Daniel and Julia, also discovered. After moving into a new area of their city, they were keen to make friends in their new neighbourhood, as well as to create some opportunities for evangelism, so they hit upon the idea of starting a book group. They made up a flier, posted it through all the doors on their street, put up a poster in the local library, and advertised it in the Facebook group for their community, with the result that twenty people turned up for the first meeting. Daniel and Julia suggested to the group that they meet once per month, with people taking it in turns to recommend a book for people to read and discuss at the next meeting. When it was their turn, they prayed and thought carefully about the best book for their purposes and picked C. S. Lewis's *The Screwtape Letters*. It's a brilliant study of the nature of evil and a very entertaining read, and Daniel and Julia found that it sparked all manner of questions about God, faith, and human nature.

Food for Thought

Creating space for discussion and questions can produce really rich soil in which conversations about Jesus can naturally grow. My

---

5 It was also from James that I learnt a neat evangelistic tool for use in bookshops: Evangelistic Book Refiling. Simply wander into your local branch of Barnes & Noble or whatever, head over to the usually cobweb-infested religion section, and find the best Christian book you can. Usually there's *something* to be found—one of C. S. Lewis's classics, for example. Pick up a couple of copies and head over to the display of bestselling books, often located in the higher-traffic front part of the shop. Now refile the books you've picked up on the first or second position in the display, and voilà! You've helped the next person perusing This Month's Bestsellers to discover a Christian book.

friend Anne, who lives in a large postindustrial city in the middle of England, discovered this as her church's members were trying to figure out how to reach the community around their new church plant. Anne hit upon the idea of organising a weekly café event in the church, with great coffee and dessert and also a question for discussion each week. Christians in the church found it easy to invite friends and neighbours, not least because the topic every week wasn't always overtly Christian but was often suggested by the audience the previous week. Over time, as the audience for Food for Thought grew and as non-Christians realised it was a fun and safe space to discuss almost every topic under the sun, Anne and the other leaders found it easier and easier to get great discussions going around the big questions of faith and life.

Wondering on the Train

Another friend of mine, Michael, has learnt to take an interest in the people he comes across and, through years of practice, to find ways to connect a conversation to Jesus. Michael told me the story of a train ride he was on in eastern Europe, travelling from northern Romania to Budapest—a journey of several hours. Sitting opposite him was a young man, and as the hours passed, they struck up a conversation. Michael discovered that the man was a university student studying environmental science.

"Why did you decide to study that particular subject?" Michael asked, and the student excitedly replied that he was deeply concerned for the environment, felt the world was facing a climate catastrophe, and thus wanted to study something that would help him make a difference.

"Why do you think we should care at all about the environment?" Michael asked.

"Because we should!" replied the student, startled that anybody would have to ask.

"I agree we should," said Michael, "but I want to know *why* you think we should. What reasons would you give?"

After thinking for a minute or so, the student replied, "Well, everyone knows we should!"

"Do they?" Michael asked. "Don't you think that if everyone *did* know that, the environment wouldn't be in the mess we're in now? Some people obviously *don't* care."

"But they should!"

"I agree! But *why* should they?"

Finally, the student admitted to Michael that he'd never actually thought about this. Michael was then able to say that he shared the student's concern for the environment but that in his case, it was because he was a Christian, believed that the world was God's good creation and gift to us, and that we therefore have a duty and responsibility to care for and look after it. That led to a conversation about faith that lasted all the way to Budapest![6]

Medicine and Mission

But of all the friends whose natural, conversational approaches to evangelism I have learnt from over the years, the one whose story continues to fascinate me the most is Peter, a family doctor working in Toronto. I first met Peter just after my wife and I had moved to Canada in 2010, and in one of our early conversations, Peter commented, "I *love* being a family doctor; it gives me so many amazing opportunities to talk to patients about my faith in Jesus." Peter went on to share how over twenty years of working as

---

6 Michael Ots tells the story—and unpacks why only Christianity offers any true basis for care for the environment—in his book *Making Sense of Life* (Leyland, UK: 10Publishing, 2021), 26.

a doctor, he had even had the privilege of praying for and leading patients to Christ, right in his consulting room.

On hearing this, I confess I was startled. A doctor, talking about faith with his patients? Praying with them? Leading them to Christ? How could that work when I knew many Christian medics—doctors, nurses, and therapists—terrified of even mentioning Jesus at work for fear of getting in trouble? In recent years, there have even been several news stories about Christian medics getting fired for merely offering to pray with patients, let alone suggesting that they follow Jesus and become Christians. What was Peter doing? How had he still got his job? Wasn't he afraid that some patient would complain that they'd come to talk about their haemorrhoids but had got heaven instead?

When I put this question to him, Peter nodded and admitted that public service jobs, like medicine, can sometimes be seen as risky territories for evangelism. When he'd first started as a doctor, sharing his faith at work had felt like tap-dancing through a minefield whilst wearing a blindfold. But then he'd noticed that as a doctor, the more he took an interest in his patients' lives, the more they would naturally open up and talk.

"Now," said Peter, "whenever I'm faced with a patient who has come to see me about something they're concerned with, I try to take the opportunity to do a little life audit with them. I'll say things like 'Tell me about your diet—are you eating well?' 'Tell me about your sleep patterns—are you sleeping well?' 'Tell me about your exercise regimen—are you exercising regularly?' And then, finally, I'll finish with something like 'Tell me about spirituality—are you making space for that in your life?'"

"And what do they say?" I asked, intrigued.

"The most common response I get is the patient saying,

'Spirituality, doctor—what do you mean?' To which I'll reply, 'Well, some people meditate; some people do yoga; in my case, I'm a Christian, so I read the Bible, pray, and go to church—those kinds of things.' And do you know what happens?"

I shook my head.

"In over 80 percent of cases (I'm a doctor; we're good at numbers) the patient will say something like 'You pray, doctor? How does that work?' And now they're asking *me* the questions, and I'm far, far freer to respond to *their* questions and find ways to bring Jesus into the discussion. Over the years, this approach has led to some amazing conversations. And I've never had a single complaint—indeed, quite the opposite. Patients will often express their gratitude that I've given them space to talk about these kinds of things in a safe setting."

The Most Overlooked Tool for Evangelism

I hope you've found some of the stories I've shared fascinating, intriguing, and even empowering. Maybe in some cases you've thought, *Hey, I could do something like that*, or perhaps a story has begun an idea brewing in your mind of a way to start conversations about Jesus among your friends and colleagues.

But I wonder if you noticed the common link between what these friends of mine have been doing. Whilst each of them had their own styles and approaches, whilst nobody was woodenly using simplistic formulae, trying to find magic bullets, or deploying cheesy shortcuts, there was something they all used.

Questions.

Whether my friends were asking questions themselves or trying to encourage others to ask them, each of the stories I shared had questions at its heart. And I want to suggest that *questions* are one of the most helpful tools available for sharing our faith, whether you have been a Christian for fifty minutes or fifty years. You can use questions to *start* conversations about your faith in Jesus, and then questions can help you *stay in* those conversations. Why are questions so powerful? Well, that is itself a really good question—and one we'll take a look at in the next chapter.

CHAPTER 5

THE POWER
OF A GOOD QUESTION

THE FAMOUS EIGHTEENTH-CENTURY French writer Voltaire is widely believed to have suggested that one should "judge a man by his questions rather than by his answers." I very much agree, although I do wonder what Voltaire might have made of some of the typical questions that get asked in the Bannister house, especially at mealtimes. In the last few days alone, I have found myself asking, "Why are you trying to inhale your spaghetti?" and "What is a dinosaur doing fighting a ninja on the dinner table?" to name but two.

More seriously, when it comes to matters of faith, my wife and I have also learnt that asking questions is a great way to inspire our kids to think about the Bible and about Jesus—to begin making their faith in Christ their own, rather than just something they do because their parents do it. There's nothing quite like a discussion about "How do we know the Bible is true?" or "Why do bad things happen like pets dying?" whilst trying to extricate a plastic tyrannosaurus rex from the salad bowl.

Similarly, when it comes to evangelism, if we can learn to ask good questions, I believe we will find it much easier to have helpful, more relaxed, and more fruitful conversations about our faith in Jesus. In particular, there are six things that good questions do really well.

Questions Create Conversations

First, questions help create conversations. It is far easier to talk about Jesus in the context of a conversation, yet we live in an age when people are increasingly losing the art. Numerous reasons have been cited for this, but one of the most likely is the time we spend endlessly obsessed with the black mirrors of our phones and tablets. Blaming digital devices for our struggle with conversation is, I admit, a bit like shooting fish in a barrel (having first glued the fish to the side and painted target symbols on them), so can we be a bit more specific? What *precisely* is the problem with technology when it comes to conversation? The key issue seems to be one of distraction, as Sherry Turkle points out in her bestselling book *Reclaiming Conversation: The Power of Talk in a Digital Age*:

> We say we turn to our phones when we're "bored." And we often find ourselves bored because we have become accustomed to a constant feed of connection, information, and entertainment. . . . There is now a word in the dictionary called "phubbing." It means maintaining eye contact while texting. My students tell me they do it all the time and it's not that hard. . . .

[All this] adds up to a flight from conversation—at least from conversation that is open-ended and spontaneous, conversation in which we play with ideas, *in which we allow ourselves to be fully present and vulnerable.*[1]

When it comes to conversation, what most people really want from their friends, family, and coworkers when they talk to them is that sense that they are being listened to, that their views matter, that they're being *heard*. What shows that we value somebody is that we give them our attention. And asking good questions—taking a genuine interest—is a brilliant way of doing that.

Of course, as Christians concerned with telling others about Jesus, we don't *just* want conversations about the weather,[2] sports, or what our kids did with plastic toys at dinner last night. We also want conversations that lean towards spiritual topics. And the good news is that people seem increasingly open to those kinds of conversations. During the early months of the COVID-19 pandemic in 2020, *The Guardian*, a British newspaper whose attitude towards Christians is traditionally akin to that of sharks towards swimmers, stunningly led with a story reporting that 33 percent of 18- to 34-year-olds had watched religious services online.[3] The *New Statesman*, another secular political magazine, went one further with an article titled "How Coronavirus Is Leading to a Religious Revival."[4] Meanwhile, the comedian Russell Brand,

---

[1] Sherry Turkle, *Reclaiming Conversation: The Power of Talk in a Digital Age* (New York: Penguin, 2015), 4, emphasis mine.

[2] It has been noted that when two British people meet, the weather usually comes up as a topic within the first minute, largely because our weather is so changeable. I have long suspected that God actually has the UK weather set to Retail Demonstration Mode: "Look! We can do rain, wind, snow, sun, hail, sleet, and plagues of frogs all in the same thirty-minute window!"

[3] Harriet Sherwood, "British Public Turn to Prayer As One in Four Tune In to Religious Services," *Guardian*, May 3, 2020, www.theguardian.com/world/2020/may/03/british-public-turn-to-prayer-as-one-in-four-tune-in-to -religious-services.

[4] Miriam Partington and Sebastian Shehadi, "How Coronavirus Is Leading to a Religious Revival," *New Statesman*, April 27, 2020, www.newstatesman.com/politics/religion/2020/04/how-coronavirus-leading-religious-revival.

wildly popular with younger audiences, posted a video to his social media feeds answering the question "Why are so many people googling 'how to pray'?" and hundreds of thousands watched.[5]

Something fascinating is going on right now. Despite increasing secularism, it only takes something like a pandemic or another national crisis for people to begin pondering life's deeper realities. And asking questions is a great way to start conversations around spiritual issues and create a space to talk about Jesus and the gospel.

Questions Avoid Drive-by Evangelism

At the same time as helping to create better conversations, questions can also help us avoid the common temptation to look for quick-fire shortcuts that allow us to do random bits of evangelism and then run away. As a teenager, it was things like sticking gospel tracts under the windscreen wipers of cars in parking lots. This plan was abandoned after some friends and I accidentally leafletted attendees at a funeral with a tract that read "Many Who Plan to Seek God at the Eleventh Hour Die at Ten-Thirty." Somebody complained to the pastor, and we made page 7 of the local newspaper for all the wrong reasons.

Technology has made drive-by evangelism much easier. We can post an evangelistic meme to our social media feed and hope that "the right person will see it," or we can email "helpful Christian videos" to our non-Christian friends and family, praying that some sort of one-click conversion might be the result. At the Q and A after one church event I spoke at, a woman asked for advice, saying, "I've been sending Christian videos to my unbelieving sister every

5 "People Are Googling Prayer Because They Are Looking for a 'Sacred Experience,' Says Russell Brand," *Christian Today*, May 10, 2020, www.christiantoday.com/article/people-are-googling-prayer-because-they-are-looking-for-a-sacred-experience-says-russell-brand/134824.htm.

week without fail for the last five years. Now she's asked me to stop sending them. What should I do?" I admitted that I was amazed it had taken 260 videos before her sister had finally had enough!

The problem with these kinds of drive-by evangelism strategies is they inadvertently treat other people like apps. We think that if we just press the right button, then bingo!—we'll get the response we're looking for. Thankfully, God himself didn't treat us like that but sent his Son, not a download, and maybe we can learn a lesson from that. Taking the time to ask good questions helps to avoid the impression that all we are interested in is throwing gospel hand grenades from a safe distance.

Questions Can Reveal Motives and Assumptions

As well as helping to *create* conversations, questions can also be helpful *within* conversations, especially if somebody raises a challenge about your faith. For example, if somebody asks, "How can you believe in God, given all the suffering in the world?"—easily one of the most common questions that people have about faith—it can be helpful to know *why* your friend has raised this issue. Is it because they're a highly sceptical atheist who has heard this is a good question to trip up Christians? Or are they asking because they have just lost a loved one to cancer? So what about replying with something like "Thanks for raising such an important question. Just out of interest, why do you ask?" If it turns out they're asking because their beloved grandmother has just died, what they may really want, rather than a ten-minute summary of your pastor's thirteen-point sermon on this topic, is sympathy and a shoulder to cry on.

You might be surprised how often personal circumstances lie behind all kinds of questions about Christianity. I once spoke to a church youth group and taught them some of the material from this chapter. A few days later, I received an email from the youth pastor, who wrote to tell me that the day after my visit, one of the youth group members had been in a science class at school. The student's classmate had said, "What are you doing in a science lab? You're a Christian, and isn't Christianity anti-science?" There were a dozen things the Christian student *could* have said (or windows he could have leapt out of to run away), but instead he politely asked where the question had come from. That opened up a conversation in which he learned that the other student had recently lost a friend in a car crash, was angry at God, and just wanted to lash out at the first Christian he came across.

So asking questions can help reveal the *motive* behind what somebody has said. But questions can also reveal *assumptions*. We can easily forget that our non-Christian friends have their own sets of beliefs about life's biggest questions, even if they've never fully thought them through or articulated them. Thus, encouraging them to explore what they really think about life, the universe, and everything can be incredibly helpful. Over the years I've found that these four questions can be used to uncover some of these basic assumptions:

- Do you think there's some kind of god, and if so, what is god like?
- What does it mean to be a human being?
- What's gone wrong with the world?
- What's the solution?[6]

---

[6] I explore these questions in more detail in Andy Bannister, *Do Muslims and Christians Worship the Same God?* (London: InterVarsity Press, 2021), especially in chapter 3.

Questions Challenge Somebody to Think

A fourth thing that questions do brilliantly is to challenge the other person in a conversation to think. Too often Christians can assume that if we are talking, say, to a secular friend, then it's *their* job to be sceptical, and it's *our* job to answer all the questions. But that can be exhausting and boring and can cause you to miss that whilst your friend has thought a bit about why they *don't* believe Christianity, they might not have spent any time considering what they *do* believe. For example, if your friend mentions they're an atheist, consider asking, "You know, atheism largely tells me what you *don't* believe—but what *do* you believe?" (After all, I don't believe in roller-skating unicorns, but if I introduced myself with that bit of information, you wouldn't learn that much about me.) Or if somebody remarks, "I don't care about religion!" it might be helpful to ask, "Well, what *do* you care most about?"

I remember on one occasion having lunch with a student who had asked if we could meet up so he could ask me "a few questions about Christianity." I hadn't realised he was using *few* in the same sense of the word as "Amazon stock a *few* items," and for two hours over burgers, he peppered me with question after question after question. I occasionally tried ineffectually to turn the conversation around to what he, as an atheist, believed but got precisely nowhere. Finally, as we walked from the restaurant to the parking lot and got to our vehicles, an idea popped into my head.

"I hope you found our conversation useful?" I asked.

"Yes, thanks for taking the time."

"And I hope, as I tried to answer all fifty-four of your questions, I treated you with respect, even though we disagreed."

"Oh yes, thank you, you've been very kind and patient."

"Great," I added, "and I must say, even though your ability to ask tough questions would make a hardened political journalist on Red Bull look like a mere amateur in comparison, you were also polite and generous in *how* you asked them."

"Thank you."

"But just one thought for you to consider. The reason I treated you with kindness was because I believe you are, as the Bible teaches, a person with value and dignity because you are made in the image of God. On the other hand, you said over lunch—three times, if I recall—that you think we are just atoms and particles. Yet you didn't treat me as just a bunch of atoms. You treated me as a person with value and dignity. In other words, you treated me on the basis of *my* beliefs, not on the basis of *your* beliefs. Don't you find that fascinating?"

For the first time in over two hours, he didn't have a quick remark in reply, and as he thought about what I'd asked, he admitted for the first time in our conversation that there were perhaps a few issues with his atheism that he hadn't considered before.

Questions Take the Pressure off You

Not only do questions help the person you're talking with think through what they believe (or don't believe), asking questions is also crucial because it takes the pressure off you. If you're not careful, you can end up doing all the talking while your friend struggles to get a word in edgeways. By asking questions, not merely do you create more of a two-way conversation, you also give yourself time to think, to pray,[7] and to listen, getting an insight into what your friend really thinks.

Furthermore, with practice, asking questions can help the person

---

7 Praying silently is best, because praying "Lord, guide this infidel before me from error to truth!" out loud while your friend speaks probably isn't the *best* approach.

you are talking with uncover spiritual truths for themselves, rather than you simply spoon-feeding them. A friend of mine was once driving to a meeting with a work colleague who remarked casually, "It doesn't matter what you believe as long as you're sincere."

Thinking quickly, my friend asked, "Can I clarify: Are you saying that as long as you believe something passionately and sincerely, you can believe *anything*?"

"That's right."

"Okay. Do you have life insurance?"

"What? Yes. But why?"

"Well, I sincerely believe I can just close my eyes and run the next red light at sixty miles per hour. I sincerely believe we'll be okay. Shall we try it?"

"Are you *insane*?"

"No. But I am *sincere*. I thought sincerity is what matters?"

Once her colleague's heart rate had decelerated to double digits, they were able to have a slightly more sensible conversation about how we know if something is true, rather than merely wishful thinking.

Questions Can Turn Arguments into Conversations

There is one final, powerful effect that questions can have—namely that they can help turn what might otherwise be an argument into a conversation. We live in an age when people are increasingly divided, with social media having trained us to take offence quickly. But arguments don't often get us very far, tending to produce more heat than light. As Christians, we want to get along with our friends like a house on fire[8] as we talk about

---

[8] Which must surely take the biscuit for the weirdest metaphor in the English language. (Although what biscuit? Who took it? And for what purpose?)

spiritual things, not descend into lobbing burning embers at each other from across the smouldering ruins.

Within the context of a conversation with a friend, it's perfectly fine to disagree, but we don't want to be *disagreeable* or to have things descend into the conversational equivalent of the Battle of the Somme. Once again, a good question can help, especially if the conversation is getting tense. Asking things like "I can see this gets you very animated; why is that?" may be helpful. On one occasion, my wife and I were having dinner with a relative who had said some extremely negative things about Christianity. My wife smiled sweetly and asked, "You seem very angry at God for somebody who doesn't believe in him. Why is that?" It turned out that our relative's scepticism derived from a deep disappointment with the way he'd been let down by some Christians in the past, and his anger at God was a mask for that.

Seven Tips for Asking Really Good Questions

So far we have explored why questions are so useful in creating space for more natural conversations about faith. We have also seen how questions are helpful in navigating those conversations, especially if our friends raise challenges or objections to what we believe. But you may be asking, *What if I'm not sure what kind of questions to ask? How can I learn to ask* better *questions?* After all, "Where did we leave the baby?" and "Should the casserole really be green?" are, grammatically, perfectly well-formed questions, but if you're asking them, arguably something has gone wrong. And there are evangelistically *bad* questions as well. One of my friends once plucked up the courage to invite a neighbour to a Christmas carol service and was delighted when they said yes. But things went slightly wrong when the greeter at the church door, spying a face he didn't recognise, met the neighbour with the words, "Welcome to St. Jude's—have you found Jesus?" The neighbour, trying to parse this weird question, replied with "Er . . . no, have you lost him?" Given that Christians sometimes already have a reputation for being a little bit odd, let's not add to that impression by asking questions that are downright weird. So how can we learn to ask better ones?

My first piece of advice is to pray. I know this sounds obvious, but sometimes it's the obvious things that we overlook, like the sunglasses on your head as you tear the house apart looking for them.[9] What precisely should we be praying for? Pray for opportunities for conversations. Pray that the Lord would create spaces in those conversations to ask questions (that way you won't feel the need to force them). Pray that the Spirit would nudge and lead you to recognise opportunities when they turn up and inspire you when they do. You might also pray over previous conversations and questions you've asked. Ask the Lord to help you discern what worked, what didn't, what you might learn for next time, and how to follow up on those that went well.

Second, learn to really listen. The best questions arise naturally out of what a friend has said, so the more carefully and attentively you listen, the more readily questions will occur to you. Sometimes because we are so passionate about Jesus and want to share him with our friends, we can talk too much and end up dominating the conversation. So remember what the Bible says. It advises us to be "quick to listen" and "slow to speak" (James 1:19). Asking questions helps us avoid twittering away and boring our friends to tears. And a great question to occasionally ask is "I think what

---

9 One of the advantages of living in the UK is that the need to play hunt-for-the-sunglasses is so rarely necessary. Our summers here are legendary, and I do mean *legendary*.

you're saying is . . . (and summarise what they've said). Did I hear you right?" The more people feel they are genuinely listened to, the more willing they may be to talk about deeper things.

Third, ask questions as a way of showing that you are taking a real interest in what your friend is saying. Simply inquiring about somebody's life, family, work, interests, and so forth can sometimes open up opportunities for much deeper things. My friend Richard is very gifted at this and is able to start conversations anywhere. A few years ago, after he and I had both spoken at a conference in Atlanta, we got a taxi to the airport, dog-tired after a really heavy day. All I wanted to do was close my eyes for twenty minutes, but Richard leapt straight into asking the taxi driver questions about his work and his family. Within ten minutes they were chatting like old friends. Toward the end of the ride, the taxi driver mentioned how his son was struggling with an issue at school, and very naturally Richard was able to say how he found, when similar issues had happened with his kids, praying about it had made a big difference. That segue to spiritual issues wasn't forced; it flowed out of the interest Richard had taken in the man's life.

Fourth, find points of connection. Especially when talking with somebody new, look for common ground—and use that to ask the other person questions and build a rapport. There's a beautiful example of this in Acts 17, where Paul is in Athens and uses the Athenians' interest in spirituality (temples, statues, altars) to open a conversation where he is then able to ask about the Altar to an Unknown God. One way I have found to do this myself is to read and watch widely, taking opportunities to sample beyond my own (often narrow) interests. Over a hundred years ago, the Baptist minister F. W. Boreham wrote a wonderful little essay, "A Slice of Infinity," in which he encourages Christians to aim at "sampling infinity" in our reading.[10] After all, if you get chatting to somebody whilst waiting at the bus stop and it turns out they are a keen angler, you'll be grateful you read *Fly Fishing* by J. R. Hartley a year back, as it gives you some points of connection you can build a conversation from.

Fifth, practice asking open rather than closed questions. A *closed* question is one that requires only a one-word answer: "Is this your dinosaur in the lettuce?" "Did you enjoy that book?" "Do you believe in God?" The person you're asking can simply say yes or no and then the conversation is over, or at least at an impasse. By contrast, *open* questions require the person to give a little more thought. For example, "What's the most important thing in life for you?" "Why are humans so fascinated by spirituality?" "What does the word *God* mean to you?" Questions like that are far more likely to open a conversation, rather than reduce it to monosyllables.

Sixth, always be ready with the next question. It's very easy in a conversation to ask a great question, see your friend really engage with it, and then suddenly find it's your turn to say something and—doh!—you're tongue-tied. So as your friend is answering and as you're listening attentively and quietly praying, think of a follow-up question to ask. Don't be worried about doing *more* of the asking and your friend doing *more* of the talking—the more you ask good questions and listen carefully, the more your friend will feel their opinion is valued and taken seriously and the readier they will be when the time comes for you to say something like "This is really interesting. You know, *I've* often thought . . ."

And finally, take your time and don't feel the pressure to go too deep too quickly. For example, consider the following exchange.

---

[10] F. W. Boreham, "A Slice of Infinity," in *Mushrooms on the Moor* (London: Epworth Press, 1928), 11–20.

Sally, a very keen Christian, is taking the trash out when she spies her next-door neighbour:

> "Hello, neighbour, how are you today?"
> "I'm doing well, Sally, thanks for asking. How are you?"
> "Great. Just taking the trash out. And I'm so grateful that Jesus has taken the trash out of my life! Tell me, have you found Jesus?"

Arguably there were probably just a few more questions and a longer conversation needed between "hello" and "have you found Jesus?" as well as possibly a slightly less cheesy introduction to spiritual things.[11] Rather than diving straight from the surface level of polite, everyday conversation to deeper spiritual things so rapidly that your friend's ears pop, practice asking questions that go deeper by degrees. Perhaps, had her neighbour had the time, Sally could have asked about how work and family were going, and if Sally, in the course of that gentle conversation, had found out her neighbour's child was unwell because they'd choked on a plastic dinosaur during the salad course at dinner last night, maybe there would have been an opportunity for Sally to offer to pray for her neighbour's family. Don't be afraid to slow down and learn to engage with people at the speed at which the Holy Spirit is working.

The Gospel as a Question

But one final thought on the subject of questions. Whilst there are many good reasons to use questions and ways to get better at asking them, there is one other massively important consideration:

---

[11] For as *Monty Python's Life of Brian* reminded us, Jesus did *not* say, "Blessed are the cheese-makers."

questions are so powerful in evangelism because the gospel is itself all about a question. Consider this well-known episode from the life of Jesus:

> Jesus and his disciples went on to the villages around Caesarea Philippi. On the way he asked them, "Who do people say I am?"
>
> They replied, "Some say John the Baptist; others say Elijah; and still others, one of the prophets."

MARK 8:27-28

I have a cinematic mind, and there are some scenes in the Bible I can picture in my head, this being one of them. I like to imagine Jesus and the disciples wandering along to another speaking engagement, the banter flowing as they're enjoying hanging out together. All of a sudden, Jesus throws a question into the mix, asking the disciples who the crowds are saying he is. And the disciples reply with some of the various rumours that are spreading around. Some people think Jesus is John the Baptist, others say he's Elijah. There was even this weird guy in Cana who thought Jesus was Elon Musk.[12] I imagine there's a bit of laughter. I mean, those crowds, right? They just don't get it! But then Jesus suddenly turns the conversation in a much more uncomfortable direction: "But what about you? . . . Who do you say I am?" (verse 29).

I imagine the laughter dying away. *It's one thing to poke fun at the crowds, but Jesus now wants to know what I think?* I envisage several disciples nudging others: "Here, Thaddaeus, you tell him!" "But I don't speak at all in the Gospels!" "Thomas, Thomas, you tell him!" "No way, dude, I'm Doubting Thomas. Or maybe I'm not?"

---

[12] To which Jesus responded, "That's two thousand years too early. That's an anachronism, lads."

Finally, Peter—good old faithful Peter, always the first to speak up, even if he doesn't get it right—pipes up, and this time he nails it: "You are the Messiah" (verse 29).

The question that Jesus put to his disciples—"Who do you say I am?"—is the gospel in a nutshell. When I'm talking with my non-Christian friends, that's the question I want to get them to, to reach a point where they are willing to read the Gospels and consider the questions "Who does Jesus think he is?" and "Do I believe him?" By learning to have good conversations and to ask good questions, we can lead people towards considering that most crucial of all questions.

Given that the gospel is, at its heart, a question—"Who do you say I am?"—it is therefore no accident that Jesus himself loved questions. In the next chapter we'll explore how Jesus used questions, see what insights we can learn from his conversations, and then discover how to apply some of Jesus' methods to some tricky real-world conversations.

CHAPTER 6

LEARNING QUESTIONS
FROM THE MASTER

ON MOST MORNINGS IN OUR HOME we try to have a short family devotional time with our kids. (Often, assorted stuffed toys and plastic action figures are also part of our diverse household congregation.) During that time, we'll look at a Bible passage together—for instance, the week I'm writing this, we've been looking at the story of Joseph in the book of Genesis and having to firmly insist to our nine-year-old that she is not allowed to dramatically act out the throwing-your-brother-into-a-pit part. During our time with the Bible, we'll often ask the kids questions to get them to think about the text, and I've noticed a pattern whereby if they suspect that we're looking for a particular answer but they don't know exactly what it is, they'll default to saying "Jesus."

I know we're not alone in this, for I recently heard of another family who, mid-devotions, were interrupted by the doorbell ringing. "Who can that be at the door?" the mother wondered out loud, to which her four-year-old daughter, still in Bible answer mode, shouted "Jesus!" She and her seven-year-old brother charged to the door, flung it open, and astonished the postman by yelling, "Mummy, it's not Jesus; it's the mail!" The four-year-old added, "Jesus probably uses the chimney, not the door." "I think you'll find that's Santa," said the postman helpfully.[1]

Whilst we may smile knowingly at such innocence and naivete, we are not immune from this same tendency in the more grown-up parts of the church. We, too, can be tempted towards simplistic soundbites, or what one of my friends calls bumper-sticker theology. I often used to wonder exactly what she meant by that until one day I noticed a car in a church parking lot, its rear end festooned with slogans that included "Chocolate Is a Food Group," "Honk If You ♥ Turtles," and "Jesus Is the Answer."

The trouble is you can't build a lot on soundbites, nor indeed on turtles. Don't misunderstand me here: I totally agree that Jesus is the answer. But the problem is that saying that and stopping there raises the question "The answer to what, precisely?" The problem with soundbite-shaped answers is they're often shallow and trite, and can give the impression that Christians are idiots, nice but dim, whose opinions shed about us much light as a one-watt clockwork light bulb. Rather than simply parroting, "Jesus Is the Answer," perhaps we need to discover the issues our friends are facing, the questions they're really asking, the challenges they're struggling with, and then figure out how to show and explain both *why* and *how* Jesus is the answer to them.

In his book *Jesus Is the Question*, Martin Copenhaver tells the

---

[1] Everyone knows that Santa doesn't deliver in person these days. Due to Elf and Safety requirements, he now uses a team of minions, or "subordinate clauses," to deliver on his behalf.

story of a friend who attended the final class ever taught by a popular Bible college professor. When the lecture ended, the class rose in a standing ovation, and as the professor hurried off the stage, he turned and paused. The applause died away as the students listened, eager to hear a final parting word. The professor looked at the students thoughtfully and said, "Just remember: Jesus is the question to all of your answers."[2]

Jesus' Love of Questions

It is absolutely fascinating to look at Jesus' own approach to questions and answers. When I speak in churches, I'm often asked to do Q and A after the talk,[3] but when you read through the Gospels carefully, you quickly discover that Jesus far preferred Q and Q and Q. The statistics are fascinating. It has been calculated that Jesus asked 307 questions in the Gospels, gets asked 183 questions, and answers at most a mere 8.[4] Which means Jesus is almost 40 times more likely to *ask* a question than to *answer* one (although that's still better odds than I encounter when asking one of my kids questions like "Who tried to paint the cat—*again*?").

Jesus asked questions of invitation ("Who are you looking for?"), questions about his identity ("Who do you say I am?"), questions about attitudes ("Why did you grumble about the splinter in your friend's eye, but not notice the log in your own?"), questions about love ("Don't even tax collectors love those who love them?"), questions about healing ("Do you want to get well?"), questions about the purpose of life ("Is life not about

---

[2] Martin B. Copenhaver, *Jesus Is the Question: The 307 Questions Jesus Asked and the 3 He Answered* (Nashville, TN: Abingdon Press, 2014), xxii.
[3] Or "Q and Eh?" if the audience is Canadian.
[4] Copenhaver, *Jesus Is the Question*, xi–xii.

more than food and clothing?"), questions about God's Kingdom ("What shall I compare the Kingdom of God to?"), questions about faith ("Do you believe I can do this?"), questions about obedience ("Why do you call me 'Lord' but don't keep my words?"), questions about discipleship ("Do you also want to leave me?"), and questions about eternal life ("All who believe in me will never die—do you believe this?").

So when it comes to asking questions ourselves in evangelism, how can we learn from Jesus, the Master Questioner? Let's take a look at four conversations Jesus had to see what we can discover.

Using a Question to Clarify Meanings and Expose Assumptions

Our first example comes from Mark 10, where we find the well-known story of Jesus and the rich young ruler. It's a slightly odd title for the episode, because nowhere does Mark tell us the man was a ruler. However, as the conversation unfolds, we discover that though he might not be a ruler in terms of leading men, he was certainly a straight lines kind of guy.

> As Jesus started on his way, a man ran up to him and fell on his knees before him. "Good teacher," he asked, "what must I do to inherit eternal life?"
>
> "Why do you call me good?" Jesus answered. "No one is good—except God alone. You know the commandments: 'You shall not murder, you shall not commit adultery, you shall not steal, you shall not give false testimony, you shall not defraud, honour your father and mother.'"
>
> "Teacher," he declared, "all these I have kept since I was a boy."

Jesus looked at him and loved him. "One thing you lack," he said. "Go, sell everything you have and give to the poor, and you will have treasure in heaven. Then come, follow me."

At this the man's face fell. He went away sad, because he had great wealth.

MARK 10:17-22

Now, you have probably heard this story many times before, but I wonder if this thought has ever struck you: What on earth was Jesus thinking when he gave that incredibly weird answer, "Why do you call me good?" Indeed, the fact that it is a totally weird answer is revealed by a simple thought experiment. Imagine that as you're reading this very paragraph, the doorbell rings. You sigh, put down the book, slightly annoyed at being torn away from the possibility of a really funny footnote,[5] and fling open the front door. Lo and behold, it's not a delivery guy dropping off a bulk order of turtle feed but your next-door neighbour. "Good neighbour," they begin hesitantly, "I wonder if I might ask: What must I do to inherit eternal life?"

Now, what answer are you *most* likely to give at this point? Perhaps if you are super confident, you might reply, "What a brilliant question! Come on in, the kettle has just boiled. I'd love to help you think about this." Perhaps if you are nervous, you might reply, "Hang on, I've got a book that can help you with that very question." And if you are fearfully knock-kneed, you might suggest, "Why don't you come along with me to church on Sunday? I bet my pastor can really help with that question."

5 Sure, that hasn't happened yet, but then British humour is designed to build up cumulatively, largely because by the time you're past the point of reasonable refund requests, it's too late.

(And then, as you bid your neighbour good evening, you quickly ring the pastor and say, "We've got a real live non-Christian coming to church on Sunday! Make sure you preach your best evangelistic sermon!")

But did you notice? You didn't instinctively reach for the answer Jesus gave to the young man: "Why do you call me good? Only God is good." So why did Jesus respond that way? Why didn't he say, "I'm the Son of God, so you're asking the right guy"? Or "Come along to the Alpha course that Peter, James, and John are leading tomorrow at the First Baptist Synagogue of Capernaum—there'll be a free loaves-and-fishes supper"? What was Jesus thinking with this whole "Why do you call me good?" business?

Well, think about this for a moment. Picture in your mind's eye a non-Christian friend. Maybe a work colleague, a classmate, or a neighbour. Now, suppose you say to your friend, "Look, I know you don't believe in God, but can you grant me a couple of things for a moment? Imagine that there *is* a God and that there *is* a heaven—just imagine for a moment. What do you think you need to do to get there?"

What do you think your typical non-Christian friend is *likely* to reply? I've tried this a few times, and by far the most common answer is "Be a good person." Most people think that if God exists, if there is an afterlife, then the way to get there is to be a decent person: to be a good citizen, be kind to others, keep your nose clean, and so on. If you're good, then God will welcome you into heaven. The most common religious position on the planet is not Christianity, Islam, or Buddhism, but Goodpersonism, the Disney view of life: all good dogs go to heaven.

And this is what the rich young man is asking Jesus. "You look like a good person, so you're going to heaven—obviously. How do

I get there?" (There's also a bit of preening going on. In verse 20, we discover that the young man is inflated like a novelty balloon at a kid's party on the helium of his own self-righteousness.) So this is the mess Jesus has to deal with. Of course he could have deflated the young man's ideas with a parable, a sermon, or a pithy one-liner, but instead Jesus does it with a question: "Why do you call me good? Only God is good."

The logic here is devastating. That question basically says to the young man, "You know what? You're absolutely right. *All* good people *do* get to go to heaven. However, there is just one itsy-bitsy problem—namely, that only God is good. Follow the steps: (1) all good people go to heaven, (2) but only God is good, (3) so who gets to go to heaven? Only God. And by the way, I'm sorry to inform you that your application to join the Trinity has been turned down."

The question also opens up a far deeper question. If the rich young man has recognised that Jesus is good, but *only* God is good, who exactly does that make Jesus? That's the real elephant in the room lurking behind Jesus' request to the young man at the end of the conversation: "Follow me."

But before that elephant, another has been exposed. Indeed, there's a whole posse of pachyderms lurking in this conversation, trying hard to blend into the wallpaper. Not least, there's the elephant of riches—that for all his questions about morality and goodness, the issue really holding the young man back is *money*, in particular his greedy attachment to it, and it's that, ultimately, that prevents him from following Jesus. And Jesus exposes that issue by asking just one question.

Jesus' conversation with the rich young man shows how asking questions can both clarify (getting to the heart of what the word *good* actually means) as well as expose (the young man's wealth obsession). And just as Jesus used a question to clarify and expose, we can do the same thing. How might we use what Jesus did here in a contemporary conversation?

Well, imagine that a friend remarks to you something like this: "How can you believe in God in a world so full of evil and suffering?" That's a *great* question, and there are many things that could be said about it (see chapter 12 for some ideas). But in the meantime, what about asking a question to expose some of the hidden assumptions behind the question? For example, you could say, "Thanks for your question—but I'm intrigued you used the word *evil*. If there is no God, how do you decide which events are *good* and which are *evil*?"

In other words, your friend has assumed that the existence of evil is a problem for Christians but hasn't considered the conundrum that if they throw God out the window, with him go many other things, not least any ability to talk about things like good and evil, other than as personal preferences. It's perfectly fine for an atheist to say, "I don't *like* violent crime"; it makes no sense for them to say, "Violent crime is *evil*." But you can unpack that whole discussion by simply asking, "Why do you call something 'evil'?"[6]

That's an example of how we might use a question like Jesus' to the rich young man to expose an assumption. But Jesus' question is also helpful for clarifying a *meaning*. People often use words quite sloppily, and this seems especially to be the case when it comes to spirituality. Folks who wouldn't dream of redefining "poison" as

---

[6] Check out chapter 8 of my book *The Atheist Who Didn't Exist, Or: the Dreadful Consequences of Bad Arguments* (Oxford: Monarch, 2015) for a longer look at the question of why we really do need God to even be able to speak of things like "good" and "bad," with the help of a meat-eating vegan, Alice in Wonderland, and Doctor Who.

"seasoning" or "do not feed the bear" as "smear your fingers with peanut butter and wiggle them through the bars" suddenly go all wobbly when it comes to words like *god*.

A few years ago, I was drinking coffee with a colleague at Toronto Pearson Airport, awaiting a flight. The café was crowded, and it wasn't long before a stranger politely asked if he could sit in the spare seat at our table. We got chatting, and it turned out he was heading to Vancouver. "What takes you out west?" I asked. Excitedly he replied that he was off to attend a spiritual conference.

"A spiritual conference?" my colleague, Rick, said. "That sounds amazing."

"Yes, it's a conference which promises to help me discover my inner divinity."

"Inert in vanity?" I repeated, as the café was noisy. "My attempts to be inert usually succeed, especially before 9:00 a.m. on a Saturday morning."

"No, no," he clarified, "inner di-vin-i-ty. The conference is all about discovering that I am god."

Now that got my attention. "Why would you call yourself god?" I asked politely.

"Oh, let me be clear," our coffee companion replied, "it's not that I'm god and you're not, but that we are *all* god. I'm god, you're god, your colleague is god—"

"Oh, I'm not sure about Rick," I added. "Trust me, I work with him."

"No, no, he really is. He's god, everybody in this café is god, every one of us is god."

It might have been tempting to make fun of this man's spiritual views, yet despite how odd they may sound, he was merely expressing a belief quite common in some Eastern religions. So was this the time to give a full-blown rebuttal, or was there a better way? There was, and my colleague found it.

"When you say *everybody* is god, you do mean *everybody*, right? Every human being who has ever lived?"

"Yes!"

"So me, Andy, that man over there with the stupid hat, every person in history—Mahatma Gandhi, Buddha, Martin Luther King Jr., Florence Nightingale—"

"Yes! Yes!"

"—Adolf Hitler, Mussolini, Stalin—"

"No! No!"

"But I thought," said Rick, "that you said *everybody* is god."

"Only the good people."

"But then who gets to decide what the word *good* means?"

We'll leave the conversation there, but my colleague's question got to the heart of the issue. Our new friend was using the word *god* really unclearly, and it just took the right question—in this case about who got to be included in this divine identity free-for-all—to pull the rug from under our friend's assumptions. We were then able, as the conversation unfolded, to gently introduce the idea that as Christians we believe that none of us is worthy of anything, let alone being confused with God, but that God in his tremendous love offers all of us the possibility of forgiveness, restoration, and adoption into his family. We're not God, but we are invited to become his sons and daughters.

Using a Question to Turn the Tables

Let's take a look at a second example in the Gospels. This time Jesus uses a question to turn the tables, taking a trap that his questioners are trying to spring on him and turning it neatly back onto them. Here's how Luke recounts the story:

> One day as Jesus was teaching the people in the temple courts and proclaiming the good news, the chief priests and the teachers of the law, together with the elders, came up to him. "Tell us by what authority you are doing these things," they said. "Who gave you this authority?"
>
> He replied, "I will also ask you a question. Tell me: John's baptism—was it from heaven, or of human origin?"
>
> They discussed it among themselves and said, "If we say, 'From heaven,' he will ask, 'Why didn't you believe him?' But if we say, 'Of human origin,' all the people will stone us, because they are persuaded that John was a prophet."
>
> So they answered, "We don't know where it was from."
>
> Jesus said, "Neither will I tell you by what authority I am doing these things."
>
> LUKE 20:1-8

Faced with this veritable crowd of questioners—the chief priests, the teachers of the law, and the elders have *all* ganged up together, presumably assuming there's safety from devastating questions in numbers—Jesus doesn't get drawn into a debate. There's no point, given these folks are not in the slightest interested in where his authority rests; they simply want to shut him down. So instead, with one question, Jesus turns the tables on them. And there are contemporary conversations where the same approach works well.

A friend was once chatting to a university student who had a question about faith, and the conversation was going well when another student, who was well known as a loudmouthed sceptic, walked past and said rudely, "Religion is a load of #*#*#* rubbish. Christianity is just a psychological crutch for those too scared to face up to life." Now there are many, many things wrong with that statement, but by far the biggest is that like many atheistic soundbites, it self-destructs. And so my friend, rather than cave in or say something equally rude, simply replied, "What if it's atheism that's the psychological crutch, clutched at by people too scared to face God or to be held to account for how they've lived their lives?"[7]

By applying a method similar to Jesus' response to the authority question, my friend was able to cause this overly confident atheist to pause for a moment, after which he laughed and remarked, "Well played, well played." That gave my friend the chance to briefly suggest that when it comes to beliefs, what matters is not how they make us *feel* but whether they are actually *true*. He then said to the atheist student, "Sometimes Christianity is far from comforting. Some days I find myself thinking the *easiest* path would be atheism—not least because it allows one to do exactly as one wishes. But I don't walk that path, simply because I don't happen to believe it's true."

Using a Question to Reveal a Contradiction or Tension

In our third example from the Gospels, we will see how Jesus on one occasion used a question to reveal an apparent contradiction in the beliefs of the religious leadership:

---

7 Similarly, my friend John Lennox had a well-known atheist snap at him, "Religion is a fairy tale for people who are scared of the dark!" John politely replied, "Maybe atheism is a fairy tale for people who are scared of the light?"

While Jesus was teaching in the temple courts, he asked, "Why do the teachers of the law say that the Messiah is the son of David? David himself, speaking by the Holy Spirit, declared:

"'The Lord said to my Lord:
    "Sit at my right hand
until I put your enemies
    under your feet."'

David himself calls him 'Lord.' How then can he be his son?"

The large crowd listened to him with delight.

MARK 12:35-37

Questions around the identity of the Messiah were lively in first-century Jerusalem, and of course, Jesus himself was well known for claiming (directly and indirectly) that he was the long-awaited saviour of Israel. To the religious elites, this went down about as well as a glass of rancid milk—hence their constant challenges about the way he and his followers behaved ("How can he be the Messiah? He heals on the Sabbath!" "He can't be the Messiah; he claims to forgive sins!" and so on). Some of the most fascinating exchanges in the Gospels come from Jesus pushing back on all of this, in word, story, and deed. But here in Mark 12 we see Jesus turn the tables and go on the offensive as he points out that it seems odd for the teachers of the law to claim the Messiah must be David's son yet is also David's Lord. Aren't they missing something somewhere?

Using a question to tease apart tensions, contradictions, or difficulties in another person's beliefs can often be a powerful step in spiritual conversations. And rather than simply saying "You're wrong!" (which may just cause your friend to get defensive), asking a question that exposes the weaknesses in their position can be far more effective. So how can we use what Jesus did here in our own conversations?

A good example comes from an experience a friend's daughter, Alice, had the other year. She had been discussing faith issues with a school friend over the lunch break and remarked that she thought the existence of moral values was a good argument for God. Her friend had cheerfully replied, "Oh, we don't need God to be good. We just each decide what's right for ourselves, and what's right for you to do may not be right for me to do. The one thing we must *never* do is tell another person they're wrong."

Bemused at this display of extreme situational ethics,[8] Alice asked a few follow-up questions. "Surely murder is wrong?"

"I couldn't say."

"Assault and battery?"[9]

"It'd be wrong for me to do it, but I couldn't say it would be wrong for you."

"Theft?"

"Couldn't say."

"Country and western music?"

"Probably wr—no, no, I couldn't say."

Finally, in desperation, Alice reached for the go-to example on these occasions: "What about what Hitler and the Nazis did?"

"Look, I find that all horrific, but I still couldn't say it was wrong."

---

8 Not to be confused with the situation of Essex, which is an English county to the east of London.

9 Defined in law as physically attacking somebody, not hitting them alternately with a salt cellar and an intensively farmed chicken.

Wow. What would *you* do faced with that kind of exchange? (And trust me, this position is not that unusual. I hear it a lot when I'm talking to students or young adults, who have often been spoon-fed this kind of insipid moral relativism since kindergarten.) Alice looked at her classmate and, indicating a plastic cup on the desk, asked, "Is that your coffee?"

"Yes, that's my grande quad nonfat cappuccino."

"Brilliant, I *love* that stuff!" And with that, Alice reached out, grabbed the coffee, and took a large gulp.

"What the heck are you doing?" her classmate protested.

"Taking your coffee," Alice replied with a grin.

"But it's *my* coffee!"

"It was. But you've convinced me that we get to decide good and evil for ourselves, that there's nothing inherently wrong with theft, and so I thought I'd take your coffee. Do you have a problem with that?"

"Well . . . yes."

"So would you say it seems to be the case that at least *some* moral values are bigger than just personal preference?"

Suffice it to say, the conversation went in a more productive direction from that point. And all Alice had done, very wittily in her case, was what Jesus did in Mark 12: pointed out, dramatically, to her friend that she seemed to believe both that morality was relative *and* that her coffee was *her* coffee.

Using a Question to Refocus the Conversation Where It Matters

Let's consider one final example of Jesus' use of questions. On this occasion, Jesus uses a question to refocus the conversation onto the issue that *really matters*. The context is a debate with his usual sparring partners, the Pharisees, who have come up with what they think is a Most Cunning Plan to deal with this recalcitrant rural rabbi:

> Then the Pharisees went out and laid plans to trap him in his words. They sent their disciples to him along with the Herodians. "Teacher," they said, "we know that you are a man of integrity and that you teach the way of God in accordance with the truth. You aren't swayed by others, because you pay no attention to who they are. Tell us then, what is your opinion? Is it right to pay the poll-tax to Caesar or not?"
>
> MATTHEW 22:15-17

The context here is that first-century Israel was an occupied land, and the Roman armies were considered by most pious Jews to be evil occupying oppressors. To pay taxes was thus to collaborate with the enemy. On the other hand, if you *didn't* pay your taxes, the Romans considered this to be an act of rebellion, which could quickly lead to arrest, torture, and execution. Roman justice was short, sharp, and brutal, and the Romans were not known for their sense of humour. The Pharisees were probably rubbing their hands with glee, thinking this was a totally brilliant trap they had sprung on Jesus.

So how does Jesus answer this booby-trapped bomb of a question? I have to admit that every time I read the story, I wish Jesus *had* answered with a clear "No, you must *never* pay tax." Wouldn't it be amazing? Every year, come tax return season, we could just write to the government and say, "I'd love to pay my taxes, but Jesus said I mustn't." I'm *sure* a rebate cheque would arrive by the following day's post.

If Jesus had said no, he'd have been arrested on the spot. If he had said yes, he'd have been instantly compromised and would have lost all authority with the crowd. The way forward becomes obvious when you realise this question is not about taxes in the first place. The Pharisees are not interested in economics, and monetary policy is not what Jesus needs to talk about here. So Jesus' approach, again based around asking questions, is brilliant:

> But Jesus, knowing their evil intent, said, "You hypocrites, why are you trying to trap me? Show me the coin used for paying the tax." They brought him a denarius, and he asked them, "Whose image is this? And whose inscription?"
> "Caesar's," they replied.
> Then he said to them, "So give back to Caesar what is Caesar's, and to God what is God's."
> MATTHEW 22:18-21

By asking those seemingly innocent questions ("Whose image is this? Whose inscription?"), Jesus is able to refocus the conversation. Sure, pay taxes when it's appropriate, but that's *not* the most important question. The most important question is not what we give to the government but what we give to God. I often wonder what would have happened had one of Jesus' questioners asked a follow-up question: "What belongs to God?" I wonder if Jesus might have replied by asking, "Whose image is on *you*?"

Using a question to refocus the conversation on the more important issue has lots of contemporary applications. Imagine you're sitting in a busy coffee shop, catching up with an old school friend whom you haven't seen for years. All is going well, when suddenly your friend looks up from her triple-shot extra-mustard macchiato and says, "Hey, you're still into that Christianity thing, aren't you? So tell me, do you think abortion is wrong?"

To your horror, she asks this question rather loudly, and you can hear the sound of other conversations in the coffee shop dying away as people lean in to listen to what you're about to say. Your heart is racing, your adrenaline is in the red zone, and you're silently praying for the Second Coming to happen (or at least a fire alarm), but no luck. You're going to have to answer. So what do you say? Of course the simple answer from Christian ethics is "Yes, it's wrong." But if you say, "Yes, it's wrong," what are your friend and all the eavesdroppers in the café going to think? Are they going to think, *This is the wisest, most reflective, most thoughtful, most progressive answer I've ever heard. Pray, tell me from where you got this wisdom, so I can seek it for myself*? Or are they going to think words like *bigot, narrow minded, fundamentalist, naive,* and so forth?

In the eyes of our non-Christian friends, what is the abortion issue all about? It's about *choice*. And what do you call people who restrict another person's choice? Our culture has a whole series of less-than-charming adjectives for them: fascists, dictators, oppressors. So a thought to consider: if answering the question that has been asked is going to give the wrong impression of God, the gospel, and you, maybe—just *maybe*—there is something wrong with the question. So why not do what Jesus did and refocus it?

For Christians, the abortion issue is about life rather than choice. So what if you responded like this? "Thanks for asking such a fascinating question. But before I try to answer it, I wonder if I might ask you something first. When do you think it's okay to take the life of a totally innocent person? What are the circumstances when you would consider that to be acceptable?" Now, unless you are having coffee with a psychopath,[10] your friend will reply that it is never okay. To which you could then say, "I agree. So the question we need to consider is, What is in the womb? Is it just a worthless collection of atoms and particles, in which case, why are we even having this conversation? Or is it a person, an innocent life, in which case, as you yourself have acknowledged, we can't just snuff it out." Now, that approach doesn't guarantee you'll have a substantive conversation, but it does make it more *likely*. Otherwise your friend won't hear "sanctity of life" but "restriction of choice."

If we follow Jesus' example and learn to ask good questions, we can often take a conversation in much more fruitful directions. Questions can help us zero in on and create space to address the things that *really* matter and not get distracted by rabbit trails and blind alleys. Remember that the right answer to the wrong question is often unhelpful.

Jesus and Questions: Some Concluding Thoughts

A few years ago, I was speaking at a conference in Canada, and after the afternoon sessions, I was sitting outside in the sunshine enjoying a quiet coffee. A young man approached me and introduced himself as one of the tech team who were running the sound system at the conference. "Have you got a few minutes?" he asked. I invited him to grab a seat, and he began to tell me his story. "I used to be a Christian," he began, "but now I'm not sure what I believe." He went on to explain how he had grown up in a very fundamentalist church, where no questions of any kind were encouraged. "If you expressed any doubts at all," he said, "you'd

---

10 This is unlikely, but if it turns out that your friend is Hannibal Lecter's little sister, just get out of the café as quickly as possible, steering clear of any sharp objects.

get shouted at and told that even *asking* questions meant you were destined for hell. So I left and considered myself an atheist. I eventually discovered an atheist group that met in the local pub and started attending, but you know what? I soon discovered they were just as fundamentalist! If you expressed doubts about something or suggested that Christians might have a point or questioned one of their favourite authors, you got shouted down. So I left that group, and now I don't know what I believe or don't believe. Any advice?"

After listening carefully, I finally replied with a question: "In all of this, what do you think of Jesus now?"

"I . . . well, I guess I miss him. I've never had a problem with Jesus. I just got the impression from the Christians I knew that Jesus had a problem with me asking questions."

Over the next few minutes, I gently pointed out that Jesus never turned away an honest questioner. Indeed, Jesus himself *loved* questions. And saying this isn't to be woolly—when Jesus replied to questions with questions, he wasn't shrugging his shoulders and saying, "Beats me!" but wanting to draw people deeper into the conversation. "Maybe you need to reread the Gospels and encounter Jesus afresh," I suggested, and I offered to put him in touch with a pastor I knew locally whose church was light-years away from the terrifyingly bonkers one he'd left.

In this chapter we've seen numerous examples of how Jesus used questions. As you read the Gospels, you'll discover hundreds more. Whether he was dealing with critics or cynics, seekers or sceptics, doubters or disciples, asking questions was a hallmark of how Jesus engaged people about faith. So how can we learn to do the same and weave more questions into our own conversations? In the next chapter, I'll introduce you to four very useful and practical questions to get you started.

CHAPTER 7

A TOOLBOX FOR EVANGELISM

I AM NOTORIOUSLY BAD AT DIY PROJECTS. Indeed, it is something of a longstanding[1] joke in our household. Among my litany of DIY failures are the sloping shelf that my kids' LEGO figures use as an indoor ski run, the time I nailed myself into the closet whilst trying to fit a sliding door, and the section of motorcycle-themed wallpaper I managed to hang upside down in my young son's bedroom, leading to questions like "Dad, do motorcyclists wear helmets because their heads are always bumping along the ground?" No wonder that every time my wife sees me wander past with a toolbox in my hand and a meaningful look on my face, she gets very nervous.

But for all of that, toolboxes are amazing things, and I'm often struck by how varied they can be. I've seen some folks with incredibly spartan toolboxes (as the old saying goes, "to the man who

---

[1] Unlike many of my projects.

has only a hammer, everything looks like a thumb"), whereas others have the most amazing collections, such as my wife's uncle who owns every tool ever made since the stone axe, and who can knock together a Boeing 787 in his shed before breakfast. For us lesser mortals, however, neither extreme is helpful: most of us need something more than a hammer and something a bit less than an entire branch of The Home Depot.

And the same is true when it comes to our evangelistic toolbox. If we are going to follow Paul's advice in Colossians 4 and "make the most of every opportunity," then it's helpful to have some tools that enable us to do that more effectively.

Just as DIY toolboxes can range from the understocked to the overly chocked, the same can sometimes happen in evangelism. It can be tempting to keep just one tool in our evangelistic toolbox—perhaps relying on magic bullets ("Every time I meet a sceptic, I give 'em a copy of my 'From Taxidermy to Christ' tract—it works every time!"), soundbites (remember "Jesus is the answer!" from the last chapter?), or scripted formulae. I recall a friend once asking me to role-play a non-Christian so he could practice "a routine" he'd learnt from a booklet. After asking my name, he then asked whether I believed in God. "I don't really care," I said, deciding to role-play an apathetic person. My friend looked really perturbed. "No! No! You're not supposed to say that! According to the script, you've got three possible answers, and depending on your answer, then I turn to the appropriate page in this booklet and follow the next steps." I gently suggested that this maybe came across as more like a Choose Your Own Adventure role-playing book[2] than any real-world evangelistic conversation I've ever known.

---

[2] "You see a sabre-toothed accountant blocking your path—do you fight it? (turn to page 24); run away? (turn to page 35); or ask if it thinks Jesus is the answer? (turn to page 316)."

But if overly spartan evangelistic toolboxes are one danger, the other is overly complicated ones. Some books on evangelism unwittingly give the impression that before you can even talk to a non-Christian, you need to master complex programmes or become the evangelistic equivalent of a chess grand master, able to tactically outwit any non-Christian who stumbles innocently across your path. Making things too complex can be a particularly sticky trap when it comes to *apologetics*, that branch of Christian theology concerned with giving reasons for the faith and answering questions or challenges.[3] Those who are mad keen on apologetics can sometimes accidentally imply that unless you can give fifty arguments for God's existence, complete with a forest of footnotes, then you'd be mad to even try evangelism.

But just as a good DIY toolbox has an appropriate (whilst not crazily exhaustive) selection of tools to get basic jobs done, so too there's a need for a well-equipped, basic, and usable-by-normal-people evangelistic toolbox. And as we saw in the last two chapters, by far the most important set of tools to include are *questions*. Indeed, I like to think of questions as something of an evangelistic multi-tool. Just as the most useful tool I own and can actually use is my trusty Swiss Army penknife,[4] so having a good set of ready-to-go questions in our evangelistic toolbox is incredibly helpful.

In the last chapter, we took a look at how Jesus used questions brilliantly, and if we're going to discover how to use questions to have more productive spiritual conversations, who better to learn from than Jesus himself? But the problem is that Jesus asked over three hundred questions in the Gospels, so where do we start?

---

3 We will dip our feet in the shallow end of the apologetics pool in chapter 12.
4 Because you never know when you'll need to loosen a screw, remove a fishhook, and extract a raspberry pip from between your teeth all at the same time.

I want to suggest to you that there are four basic questions that can be used over and over again, in a wide variety of settings. They're a great place to begin and can be the building blocks for further questions as you talk with somebody.

Four Powerful Questions

The four basic questions I keep in my evangelistic toolkit I like to call:

- The *what* question
- The *why* question
- The *wondering* question
- The *whether* question

These four questions are so useful that I have included them on a page of their own at the end of the book (see page 247), which, if you like, you can photocopy (and even put through a laminator[5]) and carry with you to help you memorise them and to remind you to use them in everyday conversations.

The *what* question is designed to unpack, challenge, or tease apart what somebody has said. In an age of soundbites, it can be helpful to encourage somebody to clarify what they mean, and we can do this by asking questions like *"What* do you mean when you say that there's no evidence that God exists?" or "I'm sorry that you feel that the church is full of hypocrites, but help me out—*what* do you mean by that exactly? Could you give me an example?"

The *why* question is helpful for encouraging somebody to explore the reasons for what they think. We live in a time when people have a tendency to say *what* they think but are not always

---

5 The device for covering things in plastic, not the contraption for dispatching baby sheep.

so good at explaining *why* they think it. So, for example, if a friend announces, "I don't believe in God," that's all well, but just putting it out there, without any reasons, doesn't get us very far. And so responding, "That's really interesting. *Why* not?" can often move a conversation deeper. Rather than being afraid when we're challenged by a sceptical friend, figuring out the right *why* question to ask can be very helpful.

Next up, the *wondering* question is invaluable when talking with somebody who doesn't have questions, objections, or challenges to what you believe—rather, they're just apathetic, agnostic, or uninterested in spiritual things. How can we start spiritual conversations with these kinds of friends? Well, we can ask questions that encourage them to *wonder* about the source of the things they care most about. For example, if your friend is deeply concerned about human rights, a question like "Have you *wondered* why as humans we're so concerned about justice?" can be a fantastic conversation starter. With a *wondering* question, you're aiming to gently nudge a conversation in a way that in time will allow you to suggest that Christianity offers a far more compelling explanation for the things your friend cares deeply about than does secularism.

And then finally, the *whether* question is a great way of pivoting a conversation at the right point towards Christianity. Rather than boldly asserting something like "I think atheism is about as much use as a chocolate teapot—you'd be a fool not to believe in God!" (which is possibly a tad confrontational), a question like "Have you ever thought *whether* it's possible that there is a God, for that would make far better sense of some things we see?" has more potential to open up a conversation. Connecting a *whether* question to a *wondering* question can be particularly helpful. After helping your friend *wonder* a bit about some of the things they care most deeply about, at the right time you can ask them to consider *whether* Jesus makes better sense of these things.

All four of these questions can be seen demonstrated by Jesus in the Gospels. For example, in the story of Jesus and the rich young man that we looked at in the last chapter, we saw Jesus use the *what* question ("What do you mean by 'good'?"). When Jesus asked the crowds about the conundrum of the Old Testament describing the Messiah both as David's son and also David's Lord, Jesus made excellent use of a *why* question ("Why do the teachers of the law say . . . ?"). Elsewhere in the Gospels, Jesus uses *wondering* questions (a good example is the Parable of the Good Samaritan in Luke 10, which gets his audience wondering about what true justice and compassion look like). And if you want to see Jesus deploy a *whether* approach, have a read of Matthew 11, where John the Baptist, languishing in prison, has sent some disciples to Jesus to ask whether he really is the Messiah. Jesus tells them to go back to John and report the deeds he has been doing, which would seem to fulfil what Isaiah had prophesied the Messiah would do. Thus John is invited to consider whether Jesus really is the promised hope of Israel.

Making the Most of Every Opportunity

In Colossians 4, the apostle Paul wrote these well-known words, encouraging the Christians in Colossae to think about how to reach their friends, neighbours, and community with the gospel:

> Devote yourselves to prayer, being watchful and thankful.
> And pray for us, too, that God may open a door for our
> message, so that we may proclaim the mystery of Christ,
> for which I am in chains. Pray that I may proclaim it

clearly, as I should. Be wise in the way you act towards outsiders; make the most of every opportunity.

COLOSSIANS 4:2-5

I am struck by the way that in this short paragraph, Paul so clearly connects three things that are essential for evangelism: prayer, opportunity, and initiative. Begin with prayer, be *devoted* in prayer—pray, pray, and pray some more. Then in answer to those prayers, look for opportunities to proclaim the gospel and do so clearly. And as you do that, take the initiative and make the most of every one of those opportunities. Having some good questions in your evangelistic toolbox will help you tremendously with that last step.

We often joke that in our house, with two inquisitive children, we are used to short words that begin with *w* and end with question marks. But we can learn a lot from kids, because they're not afraid to ask questions. We shouldn't be in evangelism, either, and so the four questions (what, why, wondering, and whether) that I've shared in this chapter are great to keep in your evangelistic toolbox. Of course, I appreciate that we've covered them at high speed, so in the next four chapters we'll look at each question in more detail, illustrating how each of them can work, along with plenty of real-world examples.

CHAPTER 8

THE *WHAT* QUESTION

AN ALL-TIME CLASSIC FAMILY MOVIE is the 1987 comedy fantasy adventure *The Princess Bride*, which tells the story of how two young lovers, Westley and Buttercup, get separated when Westley goes off to seek his fortune and ends up captured by pirates. Throw in a mix of evil, power-mad rulers, giant rats, fire-spewing swamps, political intrigue, sword battles, and a fast-moving flurry of puns and one-liners, and it's easy to see why the movie has become a classic and has spawned a million Internet memes.

Perhaps the most quoted moment from the movie is when the wicked Sicilian criminal mastermind Vizzini has kidnapped Buttercup and is being pursued by Westley, disguised at this point as the Man in Black. As Westley climbs the Cliffs of Insanity, Vizzini cuts his rope in an attempt to throw him off, but it doesn't work. In frustration, Vizzini shouts, "He didn't fall? Inconceivable!"

This is about the fifth time in as many minutes that Vizzini has used the word *inconceivable*, and his henchman, the Spanish swordsman Inigo Montoya, thoughtfully responds, "You keep using that word. I do not think it means what you think it means."

And Inigo Montoya is on to something quite profound at this point. We human beings have a tendency to casually use words in all kinds of sloppy and imprecise ways, not always stopping to consider what we actually mean. Among other things, this can sometimes lead to cultural misunderstandings, not least between Americans and Brits. Indeed, somebody once described America and Great Britain as "two nations divided by a common language." For example, Americans are often confused by the fact that to a Brit, a statement like "That's a brave idea" really means "You're absolutely insane"; "It's fine" means "Things couldn't possibly get any worse but probably will"; and "With all due respect" means "You're so clueless, you shouldn't even be allowed to run a hot dog stand."

But more seriously, the tendency to be imprecise in our words can be particularly pronounced when it comes to big topics like religion and ethics, where people have a habit of assuming that everybody in the conversation knows (and agrees on) what is meant by a word.

A *What* Question Can Bring Clarity

I recall a conversation a few years ago with a Muslim acquaintance that really first alerted me to all this. Sitting in a café drinking coffee with him, I had spent our first half hour finding out lots about what he believed, asking questions, listening, following up with further questions, and so on. And then I remember saying something like "That's really fascinating. As a Christian, what I believe is very different." But before I could unpack this further, he jumped in with "People are always trying to divide religions. But I say that Muslims and Christians—we are all brothers! We all believe in one god!"

"As you wish," I replied. "But don't you also think there are some major differences? For example, consider Jesus—"

"Ah, yes, Jesus. Peace be upon him! He believed in one god, just like Muslims and Christians believe in one god!"

"But whilst that's true, don't you think some of the differences in what you and I believe about Jesus are really quite important?"

"Inconceivable!"

And no matter how hard I tried to get a discussion going about some of the key differences between Christians and Muslims, he kept repeating the mantra that we both believe in one god, so what did those other things matter?

And then it struck me. My Muslim friend and I had both been using the word *god* without actually defining what we meant. We had both assumed that *god* was a neutral term whose meaning we both agreed upon—and the result was a conversation that had circled for over an hour.[1]

This is precisely the kind of problem where our first question— the *what* question—is so incredibly useful, for it helps keep a conversation on track by clarifying what somebody means. In so doing, you will often discover much about the beliefs and assumptions that lie behind what they have said.

Now, obviously, you don't simply woodenly interject "What?" at regular points like a parrot. Not least, it's somewhat abrupt and risks somebody looking at you and replying, "Didn't he invent

---

[1] So important is this question that I wrote a whole book about it. Check out Andy Bannister, *Do Muslims and Christians Worship the Same God?* (London: InterVarsity Press, 2021).

the steam engine?" Instead, you need to come up with a what-shaped question that will bring some clarity into the discussion. For example, now when I am talking with a Muslim about faith, I will often ask a question along these lines: "I notice we have both used the word *god* a lot in this conversation, but I wonder if it might be helpful to explain what we both mean when we say *God*. As a Muslim, what do you think God is like?"

Or sometimes I'll be more direct and say something like "I think the most important question is not 'does God exist?' (Muslims and Christians agree he does) but 'what is God like?' As a Christian, I think the Bible would say God is relational, can be known, is holy, is loving, and has supremely demonstrated all those characteristics in Jesus. What would you, as a Muslim, say you think Allah, the God of the Qur'an, is like?"

That's a much longer form of a *what* question, but it puts Jesus and his identity front and centre. You can never go wrong bringing Jesus into discussions with Muslim friends early on.

A *What* Question Can Challenge Objections

But *what* questions aren't helpful just with Muslim friends; they can also work well when talking with atheists, who can similarly bring a shipping container full of assumptions into conversations through the words they use.

Imagine, for a moment, that you are on a bus, commuting to work. It's a Monday morning, and you're minding your own business, sitting there reading your Bible. (After all, as we know, *every* Christian on public transport *always* reads the biggest, most obvious Bible they can possibly find, just so all their fellow passengers know they're a Christian.) You've also got your "I'm a Christian,

Ask Me Any Questions" hat on, the one with the flashing fish symbol on the top.

Who should get on at the next bus stop but an old friend, one you haven't seen for almost twenty years since your student days back at Midvale School for the Gifted. They immediately recognise you, sit down next to you, and notice the Bible. And the hat. Those are pretty hard to miss. And then their face contorts into a scowl, and they splutter, "Oh, you're not *still* into that religious rubbish you used to tout back at school? Seriously? I mean, nobody with any brains believes in God, right? There's no evidence at all that God exists! Religion is just a psychological crutch for those too weak to get through life on their own. And you still believe it as a grown adult? Inconceivable!"

You immediately think to yourself that this is why they're an *old* friend, since they used to come out with this stuff twenty years ago. But then you also notice that they've ranted loudly enough that everybody else around you on the bus has heard. Other people have stopped their conversations or lowered their copies of *Miniature Donkey Talk* magazine[2] and are eavesdropping on your conversation. There's even a guy opposite bringing out a bucket of popcorn from under his seat. It's *Christians versus Lions* round 2, your heart is racing, and your adrenaline needle is in the red zone—what do you say to this tirade of angry atheism that's just been launched at you?

Tempting as it may be to pull the emergency cord, force the bus to stop, and run for it, you probably ought to say *something* in reply. But you've only got a few minutes until your bus stop, so what should it be? Well, this is where a *what* question can be really

---

[2] This actually exists. People think I make these things up.

helpful. After all, your old school friend's statement was more full of assumptions than Boston Harbor was full of tea chests, so here are some angles you might try. For example, you could say, "What do you mean when you say, 'Nobody with any brains believes in God'? Aren't there lots of really smart people who believe in God?" (If they ask for examples, I often point to Francis Collins, one of the world's most famous geneticists, or the philosopher and former atheist Holly Ordway—both public intellectuals who have written widely about how their faith and their intellectual lives intersect.)

A further follow-up question could be "Just out of interest, what precisely is it about belief in God that would make it foolish? Given that the majority of human beings both now and in the past have believed in God, doesn't that seem a bit of a sweeping statement?"

Similarly, you could pick up on the throwaway remark about religion being a psychological crutch. For example, you might ask a *what* question along these lines: "What do you mean when you call religion 'a psychological crutch for those too weak to get through life on their own'? I actually find it really hard being a religious believer in a secular society—for example, atheists assault me with questions on buses! Wouldn't the default, comfortable position for those who want a quiet life be atheism?"

Yet another area ripe for a *what* question would be your friend's comment about evidence. Evidence is another classic slippery word. Figuring out exactly what somebody means by it can be like trying to catch a greasy pig on an ice rink. So ask away: "Thanks for your question. You know, I'm intrigued that you used the word *evidence* in what you just said. What do you mean by that word? What would count as evidence for you? What would you need to see that might persuade you there is something in this God thing?"

(And if you wanted to be a little edgier, you could even follow up with "What do you think is the best evidence for atheism? And what would count as evidence against it?")

Then there's your friend's remark that a "grown adult" surely wouldn't believe in God (despite the fact that a moment's googling reveals that grown adults believe in all kinds of weird things, such as homeopathy or line dancing). So perhaps another question could be "What were you getting at when you referred to 'grown adults'? Did you know, for instance, that huge numbers of Christians became followers of Jesus as adults?" (I mentioned Holly Ordway earlier.[3] Another famous example is C. S. Lewis, who was an angry atheist until his early thirties.[4]) And if you're up for a little cheekiness, it could be worth asking when your friend became an atheist. After all, if their atheism is something they've believed since they were five years old and hiding dinosaurs in the salad bowl, doesn't that make their scepticism, well, childish?

Finally, it occurs to me that just as with my Muslim friend in the earlier example, there is also a question to be asked about what the word *god* means to your sceptical school friend. You could ask a question along the lines of "You used the word *god* a couple of times there. May I ask, what do you think the word *god* means?" Your friend might think that's an obvious question, up there with "Did you know you've got your trousers on backwards?" But sometimes the obvious questions are needed because nobody else has asked them, a bit like the little child in the fairy tale who is the only one brave enough to ask, "Is it just me, or do the emperor's new clothes look a bit draughty?"

---

3 She tells her story in Holly Ordway, *Not God's Type: An Atheist Academic Lays Down Her Arms* (San Francisco: Ignatius Press, 2014).
4 See David C. Downing, *The Most Reluctant Convert: C. S. Lewis's Journey to Faith* (Downers Grove, IL: InterVarsity Press, 2002).

When I've asked this question of atheist friends, I've sometimes had answers along the lines of "God? I mean the mythical man with the big beard who lives in the clouds, throwing lightning bolts at people" or some other similarly infantile descriptions. To which you could consider following up with "So, can I clarify, you don't believe in a god like that?"

"No, of course not!"

"Excellent. Neither do I. Because that is not how the Bible describes God. In fact, the Bible says if you want to know what God is really like, you should take a look at Jesus."

Now let's be honest here. Asking any of those questions does not guarantee that your atheist friend will have a weeping conversion right there on the floor of the bus. (Although anything is possible. I have a former atheist friend who had a weeping conversion on the floor of an Australian coffee shop.) But asking a *what* question does increase the possibility of this interaction becoming a *conversation* rather than an argument and of your friend on the bus (and the others listening) thinking more deeply about faith. It also creates the opportunity that when you get off at your stop, you can say to your friend, "Hey, I've really enjoyed our conversation. Why don't we grab a coffee when you're next in town and we can talk more?"

Uncovering Smuggled Value Judgements

So far we've seen how *what* questions can be really helpful, whether we're talking with atheist friends or friends from other faith backgrounds. But there's a third way you can use a *what* question, and that's to uncover what I like to call Smuggled Value Judgements. What's a Smuggled Value Judgement? That's when somebody imports a value into a conversation despite the fact that their worldview (their belief system) doesn't really support it.

For example, I remember on one occasion chatting with an atheist colleague over lunch. At one point he glanced at the day's newspaper, which was leading with the story of some atrocity that an extremist group had just carried out in the Middle East. "Do you ever get depressed at all the evil in the world?" he remarked.

His question was itself a fascinating one, but what intrigued me more was his use of the word *evil*. After all, one cannot get away from the fact that if you are an atheist, terms like *good* and *evil* are pretty hard to justify. For an atheist, everything is ultimately just atoms and molecules, and it doesn't make much sense to label some configurations of atoms "good" and some "bad." With atheism, at best what you have is personal preference. You can say, "I don't *like* people murdering each other," but that's just a preference, like my preference for sardine-flavoured ice cream or your preference for coffee over tea.[5] By using the word *evil*, my friend has smuggled what is essentially a Christian value judgement (the Bible is very clear that *good* and *evil* are real categories) into the conversation. And a *what* question can gently expose that and use it as a basis for a spiritual conversation. For example, I could reply to my colleague, "I know how you feel—it's awful when you look at what some human beings can do to others. But may I ask you a question? What did you mean when you used the word *evil* just now? Who decides good and evil? Do we all get to make that word up for ourselves?"

Depending on how the conversation then unfolded, I would want to suggest that when *I* use the word *evil*, I'm coming at things

---

5 Although that beverage preference comes pretty close to "evil" in my book.

from a Christian perspective—for the Bible is very clear that there is evil at large in the world (and, tragically, in each of us). And fascinatingly, my atheist friend is using the word *evil* the same way—I wonder if that suggests that try as we might, we can't make sense of the world outside of Christian categories.[6]

With practice, you can learn to look for places where atheist or sceptic friends are busily smuggling Christian value judgements into conversations and—without trying to be annoyingly clever about it—you can use a *what* question to call them out on it.[7]

What Questions and Spiritual Seekers

One final situation when a *what* question can be incredibly helpful is when we encounter somebody who is spiritually open. There's an excellent example of this in the book of Acts, where in chapter 8 we read of Philip's encounter with the Ethiopian eunuch:

> Now an angel of the Lord said to Philip, "Go south to the road—the desert road—that goes down from Jerusalem to Gaza." So he started out, and on his way he met an Ethiopian eunuch, an important official in charge of all the treasury of the Kandake (which means "queen of the Ethiopians"). This man had gone to Jerusalem to worship, and on his way home was sitting in his chariot reading the Book of Isaiah the prophet. The Spirit told Philip, "Go to that chariot and stay near it."
>
> ACTS 8:26-29

---

6 If you want a very long examination of this idea throughout Western history, have a read of Tom Holland, *Dominion: The Making of the Western Mind* (London: Little, Brown, 2019). Tom was, when he wrote that book, an atheist but nevertheless was struck by how profoundly Christian the roots of the West are, especially when it comes to things like human rights and justice.

7 For more on Smuggled Value Judgements, see the two essays "The Smuggled Value Judgement" (http://www.andy bannister.net/the-smuggled-value-judgement/) and "The Magical Moral Mystery" (http://www.andybannister.net /the-magical-moral-mystery/) on my blog.

Despite encountering an open goal—the Ethiopian is already interested in Judaism and is some kind of God-fearer, as he's been in Jerusalem to worship and is reading the Scriptures—Philip doesn't launch in with a sermon but opens the dialogue with a *what* question:

> Then Philip ran up to the chariot and heard the man reading Isaiah the prophet. "Do you understand what you are reading?" Philip asked.
>
> "How can I," he said, "unless someone explains it to me?" So he invited Philip to come up and sit with him.
> ACTS 8:30-31

Philip's brilliant *what* question—"What are you reading there? Do you understand it?"—leads to a spiritual conversation in which Philip gets to show how Isaiah 53, the passage the Ethiopian was struggling to understand, was a prophecy about Jesus. And after Philip has explained all these things, the Ethiopian is so excited that he asks to be baptised.

And we too may come across people who are spiritually very close and for whom the right question can help get them over the line. A few years ago, I and a few colleagues were speaking at a week of events at a university. Every lunchtime the Christian campus groups offered a free meal and a talk on some aspect of the Christian faith. On the last day, a colleague and I got talking to a young Indian student, Aryan, whom we'd seen at every event that week.

"This has been an amazing week," he said. "I only arrived from India three months ago and had never before spoken to a Christian. But now . . . well, I can see how in a year's time or so, I might become one!"

My colleague sensed a *what* question was possibly appropriate. "What do you mean when you say, 'in a year's time'? I'm curious. Why a year?"

"Because I assume there is Christian teaching I need to learn? And some kind of induction?" Aryan looked worried. "Is there more? Some kind of exam?"

"No, no," my colleague replied, "it's much simpler. What do you think about Jesus?"

"That he was God's Son. And after the talk we just heard, that he rose from the dead. The evidence seems very strong."

"Okay. And what about you? Do you believe you've rebelled against God—what the Bible calls sin—and that you need the forgiveness that Jesus bought for you on the cross?"

"Why, yes," said Aryan quietly, "I know the life I have lived. It is not good."

"Well, you don't need to wait a year—we could pray right now, if you'd like?"

And it was a joy to pray with Aryan right there on that spot—and welcome him as a new brother in Christ, 365 days earlier than he had imagined was possible. My colleague's simple question had helped him take the few steps from spiritual seeker to follower of Jesus.

The Power of a Humble Question

Whether you're chatting with an open seeker, a friend from another faith, or an atheist colleague, a *what* question can be incredibly effective. It can help turn arguments into conversations, can encourage a friend to think beyond soundbites, and can help you feel more able to stay in a conversation as it develops.

In all of this, remember: you're not trying to win an argument, score points, or reduce a sceptical friend to a quivering wreck—this is, after all, a conversation, not a chess match. Ask questions graciously, with a twinkle in your eye, yes, but also—and more importantly—with humility in your heart. And keep practicing. Learn to look for words a friend has used that are loaded with assumptions and ask good questions about them.

So our first powerful question is the *what* question. But it's really one half of a powerful pair of questions, which with prayer and practice can transform your conversations and your confidence. In the next chapter, we'll meet the other half of the pair—the *why* question—and see how it can also make fruitful spiritual conversations seem far less inconceivable.

CHAPTER 9

THE *WHY* QUESTION

LARRY WALTERS WAS BORED. *Very* bored. His job as a long-distance truck driver filled him with despair at its utter mundaneness, and he dreamed of doing something that would lift him above the mediocrity of his everyday existence. And so, as one obviously does in these situations, Larry bought forty-some weather balloons, filled them with helium, and attached them to his favourite lawn chair, having first tied the chair to the fender of his jeep. On July 2, 1982—one of the lesser-known landmark dates in aviation history—Larry equipped himself with a pellet gun, beer, and sandwiches before strapping himself into the chair and asking a friend to cut the rope holding it to the jeep. His plan was to rise a few hundred feet, enjoy a short flight, and then shoot the balloons and descend. Alas, Larry had miscalculated somewhat and rose like a rocket into the air some 16,000 feet. In terror he dropped the gun and was left floating helplessly in the skies above Los Angeles.[1]

Eventually Larry drifted into the approach path for airliners coming in to land at Los Angeles International Airport, with one astonished captain radioing the tower to report passing "a frightened looking man in a chair." Eventually Larry's balloons followed the way of his confidence and began to deflate. As he neared the ground, he got entangled in power cables and briefly blacked out Long Beach. Safely back on terra firma, Larry was surrounded by a media scrum, microphones thrust in his face, and the press asked him, "Mr. Walters, why did you do it? *Why?*" Larry considered this for a moment and replied with the immortal words "I was bored of life—and a man can't just sit around."[2]

Despite its balloonacy, there is something about Larry's story that has always fascinated me—his courage, his tenacity, his inability to calculate lift-to-weight ratios, but especially that question the newspapers put to him. In this age of clickbait and attention-grabbing headlines above articles with little substance, the media are not especially famed for their ability to ask insightful questions, but those journalists nailed it. "Why did you do it?" *Why* questions are some of the most powerful we can ask. They get the other person really thinking, and they can dig into the deepest foundations of what makes another person tick. They can reveal somebody's beliefs, desires, and worldview. And that's why (pardon the pun) the *why* question is the second powerful question in our toolbox we can use in evangelism.

---

[1] See "Truck Driver Takes to Skies in a Lawn Chair," *New York Times*, July 3, 1982, www.nytimes.com/1982/07/03/us/truck-driver-takes-to-skies-in-a-lawn-chair.html. His "vehicle," which Larry christened *Inspiration I*, ended up in the National Air and Space Museum. See "How the Balloon-Borne 'Flying Lawn Chair' Got into the Smithsonian," *Air & Space Magazine*, September 2019, www.airspacemag.com/airspacemag/flying-lawn-chair-180972974/.

[2] Regional safety inspectors were far less impressed, and a spokesperson announced, "We know he broke some part of the Federal Aviation Act, and as soon as we decide which part it is, some type of charge will be filed."

Let's face it: we live in an age that seems to get more superficial by the day. Given a choice, many people would rather read a story about some airheaded Hollywood celebrity's view on why lip gloss helps fight climate change than an in-depth, long-form, thoughtful article on a political issue. Our digital devices have taught us to repetitively scroll and click, endlessly distracted ("Look! A squirrel!") by the next interesting factoid, rather than to think deeply. And layered on top of that, our culture is ever more driven by feelings and emotions than by thought, reason, and argument. All of that can make it harder for Christians to get a hearing for what we want to share about Jesus and the gospel.

But the good news is that for all the superficiality and triviality that riddles our culture like termites in a log, people still know deep down that there are *some* areas of life where reasons and facts really do matter. When the doctor says, "I'd like to remove both your kidneys and plumb your small intestine into your left ear," or the pilot says, "I'm going to turn both the engines off," or the small child says, "Daddy, I've just borrowed the chain saw; I'll be in my bedroom," everybody's instinctive reaction is still to ask why (in the last case, whilst ascending the stairs three at a time).

Our culture hasn't *totally* forgotten the need to ask *why* questions. It's just that these questions have become neglected when it comes to religious or ethical concerns. Partly because people are afraid of disagreement, partly because we've privatised religion and made it a personal preference, our culture has disconnected spirituality from truth and made religion a *feelings* topic rather than a *truth* topic. So one of our jobs in sharing our faith with our friends is to reconnect them.

And the *why* question is a brilliant and easy way to do this. Let me show you how it works with some examples.

Using a *Why* Question to Defuse a Challenge

Imagine a scenario with me for a few minutes. It's Monday morning and you're busy at work, sitting at your desk, minding your own business, working on that spreadsheet the boss wanted tracking miniature donkey exports to Azerbaijan for the last quarter. Suddenly a colleague walks past and stops as he sees the big, black Bible on the corner of your desk. (As we know, *every* Christian at work *always* keeps the biggest, most obvious Bible they can possibly find on their desk, just so all their colleagues know that they're a Christian. You're so keen, you've even got one of those giant Victorian leather-bound preaching Bibles, complete with the wooden reading stand shaped like an eagle underneath it. Nobody is missing *this* Bible!) Anyway, seeing your Bible, your colleague sneeringly remarks, "A Bible? *Really?* Come on, nobody takes that thing seriously these days. The Bible's just an ancient collection of fairy tales, riddled with contradictions."

As their words die away, you notice that their little rant was loud enough to have attracted attention—you work in an open-plan office[3]—and you can see other colleagues peering around from their workstations to listen in to some free Monday-morning entertainment. One or two are even fetching buckets of popcorn from under their desks so they can munch as they watch *Christians versus Lions* round 3.

Oh, and to make things worse, the colleague who made the remark isn't just *any* colleague. They are a senior manager, who also happens to be the big boss's brother-in-law (the company you work for doesn't promote family values so much as family members).

So what do you say? How do you respond? Pray for a fire drill?

---

3 "Open-plan office" being management speak for "we're too cheap to afford drywall."

Resign on the spot and head out to Azerbaijan as a missionary? Well, this is a perfect opportunity to put the *why* question to good use, because your colleague's statement has assumed an awful lot, assumptions they haven't given any reasons for—and the *why* question can help you challenge them in a way that is gracious as well as clear. For example, you could reply, "Thanks for that—I've often met others who hold a similar opinion. But I wonder if you could help me out: Why in particular do you think that about the Bible? Was there some specific evidence that led you to that conclusion?"

What you've done with that question is, in a friendly way, pointed out that your colleague has given you a conclusion (the Bible is a collection of fairy tales) but hasn't told you *why* they believe that to be the case. As my old maths teacher used to drum into us as students, "Show your working!" In other words, we need to know not just *what* somebody thinks but *why* they think it.

Alternatively, you could zero in on your colleague's other comment about the Bible as you say, "You're not the first person I've heard say they think the Bible is 'riddled with contradictions.' But may I ask, why do you say that? Is there a particular example in the Bible you were thinking of?"

In their comment about contradictions, your colleague has made one of those typically sweeping statements that humans are so fond of (e.g., "You can *never* trust a lawyer"; "*All* British men are unusually tall, dark, and handsome"), but these kinds of remarks are naturally sloppy, so it's helpful to clarify by asking the person to illustrate what they mean. (For example, you could challenge the latter claim by looking at the author photo on the back of this book.)

What I've found over the years when I've heard sceptical friends make these kinds of comments and I've asked a *why* question is that one of two things happens. The first (and most likely possibility) is that your colleague has *never* thought about these things. They simply heard some cynical celebrity atheist make a comment on a YouTube video, or they read it on Twitter or something, and they're parroting warmed-over, secondhand scepticism. In which case their response may be something like "Well, everybody knows." Which is shorthand for "I haven't got the first clue what to say next, so I'd better just bluster." Of course, the problem is there are lots of things that "everybody knew" that turned out to be wrong. Indeed, just the other day I caught one of my kids trying to remove a stuck piece of bread from the toaster with a carving knife, and their defence was "Dad, everybody knows this is the way to do it." To which I replied, "Well, as long as 'everybody' is willing to chip in for a new toaster, that's fine!"

If your colleague reaches for a variant of "everybody knows," you might consider following up by saying something like "I appreciate that you personally believe this. But given that there are over two billion Christians in the world, I'm not sure 'everybody' does agree with you. And I wonder if, when it comes to spiritual questions, perhaps we need more than just a hunch or unquestioningly following what we think the crowd believes. I happen to think there are some very good reasons why the Bible is trustworthy—I'd be happy to grab a coffee sometime and tell you a bit more."

But there's a second possibility—namely, that your colleague might actually have a particular issue with the Bible in mind. And so when you ask them to give an example, they are able to give you something substantive. For example, I remember on one occasion talking to a man who had grown up in the church, had stumbled across some difficulties with the Bible, and had asked his youth leaders for help, and they'd simply shrugged and told him not to worry. Well, he *did* worry, and the worry became a gnawing doubt, and the gnawing doubts festered, and now, in his thirties, he was a bit of a sceptic. So when I asked him, "Could you give me an example?" he was ready and able.

If that happens, brilliant! Rather than dealing with vagaries, you're now tackling a specific issue. And it may well be that you *know* the answer to the issue in question—in which case, don't be afraid to share it. Personalising the answer a bit can often make things more accessible. Rather than "Great question! Stand there while I download my thirty-minute answer on you that I learnt from a book I read on a donkey-riding vacation in Azerbaijan last year," it's much more effective to say, "That's a great question. I remember puzzling over that passage in the Bible myself. But then I read a really helpful article, which explained . . ."

But what if you *don't* know the answer to the issue they've raised? What if your instinctive reaction is to panic and think, *Heck, that's a toughie?* Well, again, no problem. Look on this as a great opportunity to fulfil the exhortation in 1 Peter 3:15 to "be prepared." You can say something like this to your colleague: "Thanks for sharing that. And I confess, I don't immediately know the answer. But leave it with me—I'm a Christian who likes to be thought-through in their faith, so I'll do some digging and get back to you."

And then be true to your word. Take the time to find the answer. Do some googling, read a book, ask a more experienced Christian friend, or ask your pastor. And once you've researched the answer, that gives you a brilliant follow-up opportunity, as you can search out your colleague, knock on their door, and say, "Thanks so much for that question you asked about the Bible last week. As I promised,

I did some research for you, and it turns out there's a really good answer. Do you have five minutes? I'd love to share it with you."

There's a chance the door might get shut on you. But there's also a strong chance, if you've done all this in a friendly way, that your colleague may say, "Okay, what have you got?" And off you go! All this from responding to their initial challenge not with fear or hostility but by asking a *why* question.

Making Everybody in the Conversation Do Some Work

It's not just sceptical atheist friends who have questions about the Bible. The same is true of our friends from other faiths. I recall one occasion when I had been speaking on a university campus, giving a lunchtime talk about the historical evidence for the resurrection. At the end, a student came up to me and asked if I had two minutes for a quick question. "Sure," I said, "what's the question?"

"Well, I enjoyed your talk immensely," he replied, "but here's the thing—in it you quoted the Bible a few times. But I'm a Muslim, and as Muslims we are taught that the Bible has been corrupted and is not reliable, that it is the Qur'an that is God's unchangeable word. Tell me, why should I, as a Muslim, trust the Bible?"

I remember looking at him thoughtfully and replying, "I thought you said you had a two-minute question. This is probably at least a *twenty*-minute conversation. Have you got time for a coffee?"

We found the nearest coffee shop, one of those overpriced establishments that charge you an eye-watering amount of money, mispronounce your name loudly, and then burn the coffee, but sometimes needs must. As we sipped our coffees and introduced ourselves properly, I considered my response. Because Islam is my area of academic study, it could have been tempting to give my new friend a mini lecture—but here's the thing: *even if you know the answer inside out and backwards, it can still be helpful to lead with a* why *question.* And so I did: "Faisal, let me ask you this: *Why* do you think the Bible has been corrupted?"

"Well, that's what our leaders tell us."

"Okay, but if I said to you that the Qur'an has been corrupted and is unreliable, what would you say?"

"I'd ask you to prove it!"

"Exactly. Do you see my point?"

Faisal sipped his coffee thoughtfully. And so I took the opportunity to press further: "Have you thought about *why* God might allow Scripture to become corrupted? You believe that God is all-powerful and most compassionate, right?"

"Yes, this is what the Qur'an teaches."

"The Bible says the same. So here's my question: *Why* would an all-powerful and compassionate God let this happen? Don't we *need* Scripture to tell us the truth about him? If Allah has allowed this to happen to the Bible, that suggests to me that either he *couldn't* preserve it (he wasn't powerful enough) or that Allah couldn't be bothered (he doesn't really care). Which of those options do you think might be the reason?"

Faisal was looking increasingly uncomfortable. "I guess I hadn't thought about some of this," he admitted.

"Fair enough," I replied. "And look—as religious people, sometimes we can uncritically listen to what our leaders say but forget to ask, 'Why?' and 'What's the evidence?' So how's this for a suggestion: instead of criticising each other's Scriptures, why don't we talk about what our Scriptures *actually* say. We could start with Jesus. Why don't you tell me what the Qur'an says about him, and then I'll share a bit more about what the Bible says. How would that be?"

From there, what had begun as a request for "two minutes"

opened into a two-hour conversation during which I had the opportunity to share a great deal of Jesus' teaching, claims about himself, and more about his death and resurrection, as Faisal had never read any of the Bible for himself. And it all grew from a *why* question.

Using a *Why* Question with Ethical Challenges

Another way that a *why* question can prove valuable is when it comes to ethical challenges to Christianity. It probably has not escaped your attention that in recent years the objections people have to Christian faith have subtly shifted from "Christianity isn't true!" to "Christianity is *bad*!" Whereas once somebody might have said they couldn't consider Christianity because they believed science had buried God, now people are increasingly saying they couldn't consider Christianity because of what it teaches about sexuality. I have lost count of how many Christians I have met who have been indirectly (or often directly!) accused of being homophobic, transphobic, or some other terrifying multisyllabic adjective because of what the questioner thinks they believe about LGBTQIA+ issues.

Once again, having the *why* question in your evangelistic toolkit can be very helpful, as it can both open up and help you stay in a conversation which strays into this territory. A friend of mine shared a story where this had happened. She had been chatting with a work colleague about their respective weekends and had happened to mention that she'd been to church. Immediately her colleague's demeanour changed, and she became notably frostier. My friend enquired if anything was the matter.

"I didn't have you down as one of those religious types, that's all."

"*What* do you mean?" my friend asked (using the first of our toolbox questions).

"I just don't have a lot of time for Christians, sorry," her colleague replied.

"You don't need to apologise—but I'd like to hear *why*. Have you had a bad experience with Christians?"

"Not especially. But why would I want anything to do with Christians when they don't want anything to do with me?"

My friend pressed a bit further, and her colleague opened up a bit and explained how she was gay and was in a same-sex marriage, but everything she'd heard about "evangelical Christians" (a phrase that to her definitely needed the scare quotes) suggested that Christians hated gay people.

"I'm sorry to hear that's your impression of Christians," my friend replied, "but perhaps we agree on more than you think. It sounds like you think sex and sexuality are really important— almost sacred, even?"

"Well, I wouldn't use that exact word, but yes, very much so. This is my identity we're talking about."

"Okay," my friend continued, "well, Christians also believe that sex really matters. Not least because we believe that God created it for some powerful reasons. For example, marriage and sexual intimacy is one of the major metaphors the Bible uses for the relationship between God and his people. That's why I think sex matters. But I'd love to know why you think sex matters."

"What do you mean?"

"Well, if you're an atheist, aren't you pretty much committed to the view that sex is tied in with survival and reproduction—that all our genes care about is that we pass on our DNA to the next generation? Why do you think how we *feel* about our sexual identity matters, at least on the basis of atheism?"

Her colleague thought for a long while before replying, "I confess I've never thought about that."

"But it's a good question, wouldn't you say?" my friend asked. "Indeed, I'd want to suggest that the fact that we need more than just food and reproduction—that we also need to ask the *why* questions, not least about identity—suggests humans are wired for something bigger. And I'd want to encourage you to consider the idea that maybe there's something to the Bible's teaching that all of us—no matter our race, gender, or sexuality—are made in God's image and will never find ultimate happiness until we make our peace with him."

Now, again, I'd love to say that the conversation ended with my friend's colleague in weeping repentance on the floor. But it did lead to more conversations, much more friendly than how the first began, and in time it enabled my friend to give her colleague a book as a gift—*A War of Loves*, by another friend of mine, David Bennett. That's an astonishing autobiography of how David, an atheist gay-rights activist and avid hater of all things Christian, powerfully encountered Christ. It's hard for anyone to read it and not come away deeply moved that for all the mistakes Christians have sometimes made in how we've handled this topic, Jesus truly is good news for LGBTQIA+ people, and the sacrifices involved in following him are worth it.

The Importance of Foundations

One of my kids' favourite games is Jenga, the tower-building game where you try to balance ever more wooden blocks atop an increasingly wobbly tower. (We had friends who bought a garden version of Jenga, each block about 60 centimeters long and weighing over a pound, which adds the excitement of fractures and mild concussions to an already nail-biting game.) One thing you learn very quickly when you play Jenga is the importance of a good foundation. If you start your tower on a thick-piled carpet rather than a wooden floor, you're going to get into trouble fast.

And beliefs are rather like those towers of wooden blocks. They need foundations, they need to be supported by other beliefs, and sometimes it's only when somebody comes along with a well-placed *why* question that it turns out your tower is shakier than you realised. That's why it's important we listen carefully to our friends—listen for when they express a belief or opinion, an idea or an argument—and be willing to politely ask *why* they believe it.

At the same time, it's important that as Christians we think through our beliefs, that we be able to "give the reason for [our] hope," as 1 Peter 3:15 reminds us. Sometimes in the church we are tempted to neglect this, or we lean towards giving how-shaped answers to why-shaped questions. What do I mean?

Well, imagine somebody asks you, "Why are you a Christian?" Switching seamlessly into Testimony Mode™, you reply, "I'm so glad you asked! Well, many years ago I worked at this office and I became friends with the guy in the cubicle next to mine. We started hanging out together—we both played cricket a bit—and I discovered he was a Christian. One day, he invited me to a course at his church called Alpha. I went along, and the pasta was lovely, the people were very friendly, they explained Christianity to me, and I became a Christian."

So what's the problem here? That's a perfectly acceptable testimony, right? Well, the problem is that you've told a story about *how* you became a Christian, when the question your friend had asked was *why* you're a Christian. You see, we could rerun the story above: "I'm so glad you asked! Well, many years ago I worked at this office and I became friends with the guy in the cubicle next to mine. We started hanging out together—we both played cricket a bit—and I discovered he was a Hindu. One day, he invited me to a course at the local Hindu temple. I went along, and the curry was lovely, the people were very friendly, they explained Hinduism to me, and I became a Hindu."

Thought-provoking, right? You see, if the answer to the question "Why are you a Christian?" is the story of *how* you became one, there's a problem, because everybody in our culture has fascinating personal stories—our Hindu friends, our Muslim friends, our secular friends. And if all we have to offer people is a personal story, what reason do they have for taking it seriously? At best we risk somebody saying, "That's great *for you!*" Don't mishear me: I'm not saying there's anything wrong with testimonies. I'm simply encouraging us to go further than *just* testimony. If we can also learn to gently and confidently explain *why* we are followers of Jesus—if we can back up our personal stories with some persuasive reasons—then that can be a very powerful combination indeed.

Maybe take some time right now to think about the reasons why you're a Christian, why you're following Jesus today, right now. What would be, as it were, your "elevator pitch" for Christianity? Perhaps share it with a Christian friend and get their feedback—and encourage them to ask you *why* questions at appropriate points.

So far, we've met the *what* and the *why* questions. And they're great for engaging both sceptics and those from other faiths. But what if you don't have sceptical friends? What if all your friends are apathetic and uninterested? What if trying to start spiritual conversations with your colleagues is like trying to nail Scotch mist to the wall? That's where our next question—the *wondering* question—can be especially helpful.

CHAPTER 10

THE *WONDERING* QUESTION

As the parent of two small children, one of the things that regularly strikes me (apart from rubber bullets fired by my six-year-old from one of the many toy guns in his armoury[1]) is the capacity they have for wonder. Children have a natural gift of finding something magical, exciting, and wondrous almost anywhere, whether in an insect ("Look, Mum! I found you a *huge* spider!"), or in a piece of broken pottery discovered whilst digging up Dad's prized tomato plants, or in the patterns made by the frost on the windowpane.

When we grow older, we sometimes neglect wonder, drifting instead into seeing the world as mundane. One of my favourite writers, F. W. Boreham, put it this way:

---

[1] I repeatedly have to tell him that a Nerf is a Nerf.

> We have an ugly habit of regarding one miracle as
> marvellous, but a million miracles as commonplace. If,
> once in a century, the almond, the hawthorn, or the gorse
> sprang to life again, people would flock from every corner
> of the globe to behold the miracle. But because every
> springtime every tree bursts into tender leaf and delicate
> flower, we see nothing extraordinary in it.[2]

This taking-of-the-world-for-granted is easy to do when we live in a highly secular culture—where if something can't be measured, weighed, or digitised, then it's considered to be less significant. Whereas once our culture was like a two-storey house—with a downstairs, everyday world but with most people taking for granted there was also an upstairs, supernatural, spiritual realm—now we're encouraged to live in a bungalow. But whilst John Lennon could casually sing, "Above us, only sky," this view has some consequences—not least that it's a short hop, skip, and jump from the world becoming *desacralised* to its becoming *disenchanted*, with childlike wonder at the magic of the world considered, well, childish. The spider of wonder has met the rolled-up newspaper of cynicism.

But just like the bubble under the wallpaper that simply pops up elsewhere when you attempt to flatten it, so our capacity for wonder refuses to be easily squished, even when people would not describe themselves as religious. I recently listened to a dialogue between the Canadian psychologist Jordan Peterson, who is famously vague on the question of whether he believes in God, and the British psychologist, broadcaster, and committed atheist

---

[2] F. W. Boreham, *A Reel of Rainbow* (London: Epworth Press, 1920), 74.

Susan Blackmore. Halfway through their conversation, Susan made this intriguing remark:

> I'm much more in recent years in the habit of waking up in the morning (even if it's raining in January in England), and looking out, and going "Oh!" and it's a feeling of gratitude. Not gratitude towards god, or towards anybody, or anything, just free-floating gratitude. . . .
>
> This morning, for example, I looked out and it was so green. We've had frosts and it's been white the last few days, and it was green this morning. And it was just gratitude to the universe, if you like. It's not really "god" because it's not a creator, it's not anything I can pray to.[3]

There's an obvious question here, and Jordan asked it: "Why feel gratitude towards it then?" To which Susan responded, "I don't know."

I think what Susan was struggling with is that gratitude is closely linked to wonder, and if one is attempting to live in a universe where science can explain everything, where the supernatural is denied, and where all that exists consists of atoms, particles, and matter, then gratitude doesn't really fit. Yet despite that, when Susan threw back the bedroom curtains and looked out at the beauty of the world, her instinctive reaction was nevertheless to say, "Oh!" Indeed, as somebody once remarked, the greatest problem for many people is not that they have nothing to be thankful *for* but that they have no one to be thankful *to*.

---

3 "The Big Conversation, Episode 1: Jordan Peterson vs. Susan Blackmore, Do We Need God to Make Sense of Life?", interview by Justin Brierley, accessed January 20, 2022, video, https://www.youtube.com/watch?v=syP-OtdClho. The snippets I quote can be found at 31:40 and 32:31.

So, how does this help us when it comes to evangelism? Let's find out, by borrowing an illustration from writer and novelist C. S. Lewis.

A Visit to C. S. Lewis's Toolshed

In a 1945 newspaper article, Lewis described the following scene:

> I was standing today in the dark toolshed. The sun was shining outside and through the crack at the top of the door there came a sunbeam. From where I stood that beam of light, with the specks of dust floating in it, was the most striking thing in the place. Everything else was almost pitch-black. I was seeing the beam, not seeing things by it.
>
> Then I moved, so that the beam fell on my eyes. Instantly the whole previous picture vanished. I saw no toolshed, and (above all) no beam. Instead I saw, framed in the irregular cranny at the top of the door, green leaves moving on the branches of a tree outside and beyond that, 90 odd million miles away, the sun. Looking along the beam, and looking at the beam are very different experiences.[4]

Personally, I'm wonder-struck that Lewis had a garden shed he could actually stand in. Ours is so full—of tools, rusting bicycles, buckets of old bits of pottery my kids won't let me toss out, two dozen old paint tins, and twenty years of assorted bric-a-brac, all tied together by a garden hose that miraculously unrolls itself every

---

[4] C. S. Lewis, "Meditation in a Toolshed," *First and Second Things: Essays on Theology and Ethics* (London: Collins Fount, 1985), 19–24, citing 50.

time I shut the door—that I think any self-respecting sunbeam would take one look and hightail it out again. But that aside, it's a very vivid picture, and one that Lewis develops to contrast the difference between having an experience and seeing it from the outside. For example, someone may experience the joy of being in love, but a scientist might explain it away as merely a chemical reaction caused by their genes.

However, I think there's another way of developing the sunbeam-in-the-suspiciously-empty-I-bet-he-has-a-second-one-stuffed-to-the-gunwales-shed illustration in a way that sets up our third question, the *wondering* question. Let's return to that shed for a moment. There you are, in the dark, and there's the sunbeam, slanting down through a crack at the top of the door. It occurs to me that there are actually *three* ways you can think about this.

First, you could indeed look *at* the beam itself. You can think to yourself how pretty it is, how enchantingly the dust motes dance in the light. If you were of a poetic frame of mind, perhaps you'd be inspired to write a little ode about it, excited at the prospect of how many words rhyme with *beam* as opposed to *walrus*.[5]

Second, you could look *through* the beam entirely—ignoring it and focussing on the shed wall beyond it. Or, if one was of a secular frame of mind, you could even try and explain away the beam as nothing more than a bunch of excitable photons. The writer Anthony Esolen playfully parodies this philosophy:

> [For a committed atheist] it is best to keep the word
> "*only*" ready in the arsenal at all times. The flame of
> the sky at sunset is "only" the part of the spectrum

---

5 "Nothing rhymes with walrus," I explained to my nine-year-old. She looked thoughtful before replying, "No, it doesn't."

that penetrates the atmosphere at that angle . . . it is
"only" something or other material that scientists know
about . . . or at least somebody knows all about them in
some Important Places. Beauty is "only" a neurological
tic, or a personal opinion.[6]

And third, you could—as Lewis did in the original parable—
turn and look *along* the beam and see the garden through the gap
in the shed door, the clouds in the sky, and across millions of miles
of space, the sun itself, burning brightly at the centre of our solar
system, the source of the light we take for granted.

So let's now apply this to Susan Blackmore, wrestling with her
experience of gratitude. When it comes to that experience, she can
look *at* it: "I'm feeling grateful—isn't it lovely!" Or she can look
through it: "Gratitude is just a chemical reaction in my brain; it's
just a bunch of happy neurons, merely a feeling." But where things
get interesting is if Susan could have been persuaded to turn and
look *along* her experience—what might she have seen? If gratitude
is, as it were, a beam of light piercing into the darkness of our
everyday existence, where does it originate? If the sun lies at the
end of the sunbeam in the shed, what's the source that lies at the
end of something like gratitude?

And this is where the *wondering* question is incredibly powerful,
because it equips us to take things that really matter to our friends
and get them thinking about their source. No matter what they
say their beliefs about spirituality and religion are, your friends,
family, and colleagues—even the most dyed-in-the-wool secular
ones among them—will care passionately about things like justice,

---

[6] Anthony Esolen, *Ten Ways to Destroy the Imagination of Your Child* (Wilmington, DE: Intercollegiate Studies
Institute, 2010), 236.

beauty, joy, meaning, human rights, truth, love, consciousness, free will, gratitude, and happiness. And what all these experiences, longings, and desires have in common is that none of them fit well into a godless world. As the poet Robert Frost famously wrote:

> *We dance round in a ring and suppose,*
> *But the Secret sits in the middle and knows.*[7]

With a *wondering* question what we want to do is find the things that your friends care deeply about, that animate them, and ask questions that encourage them to think about where those experiences point. But enough of the theory. Let's see what this approach looks like in action.

Three Examples of "Wondering Out Loud"

An excellent example of how a *wondering* question can open up a conversation comes from my friend Michael Ots, whom we met back in chapter 4. On one occasion, Michael was chatting with a student he had met who, on discovering that Michael was a Christian, bluntly remarked, "I'm not into God." Now, that's the kind of statement that could lock, bolt, and nail planks over the door to a spiritual conversation if you let it, but Michael thought that whilst the front entrance might be shut, there might still be a side door into a conversation.[8] So he replied, "Fair enough. So what *are* you into?"

"I'm into love," the student replied.

"That's great," Michael said. "What do you think love actually *is*?"

---

[7] Robert Frost, "The Secret Sits" in *The Poetry of Robert Frost: The Collected Poems*, ed. Edward Connery Lathem (New York: Henry Holt and Company, 1979), 362.

[8] The story is told in Michael Ots, *Making Sense of Life* (Leyland, UK: 10Publishing, 2021), 152–153.

The student thought for a minute before responding, "I'm not sure."

"Well, how's this for a definition?" Michael said. "Love is a chemical reaction that has evolved in our brains to make us attracted to people, typically of the opposite sex, so that we reproduce and pass on our DNA."

"That's rubbish!" the student replied. (Her boyfriend was standing next to her.) "That's not love."

Michael was then able to ask whether the student had ever wondered why she thought love was so important and why, if she really was an atheist, a purely materialistic answer wasn't satisfying. After all, if there really is a God, who has purposefully created us with the intention that we would learn to love him and love each other, that offers a much richer explanation of love than the idea that it's just a few genes jostling about with their eye on the survival of the species.

In my case, as somebody who loves hiking and climbing in the mountains, I have found that it is the topic of beauty that offers lots of opportunities to ask *wondering* questions. One conversation I particularly remember occurred a few years ago when I was in the United States. I was visiting a friend who works at *National Geographic*, a magazine well-known for its commitment to a purely secular, material view of the world but also famous for the beautiful photography and artwork that graces its pages. As we sat eating lunch, one of my friend's colleagues happened to be at the same table, and my friend introduced us and said I was in town to give a talk at a local church that evening. His colleague made a slightly derogatory remark about religious belief, so I asked whether he would describe himself as an atheist. He said he would, so I replied, "I find it intriguing that an atheist would work somewhere like *National Geographic*."

"Why?" he asked, puzzled.

"Well, isn't this a magazine famed for its love of natural beauty? Look at all those gorgeous framed magazine covers on the wall behind you."

"Yes, it is. It's one reason I enjoy working here."

"But haven't you ever wondered about beauty? I mean, it's a bit odd, when you think about it, if atheism is true. Why do we have this instinctive reaction to natural beauty? Have you wondered why it moves us, inspires us, why we feel the need to paint, photograph, draw, or write about it?"

"I guess I've never really thought about that," he admitted.

"I just wonder if beauty is something that actually fits a little bit better into a world with a God behind it," I continued. "If God is the Creator who has designed us to respond to art and beauty— if, as the Bible puts it, God 'has made everything beautiful in its time. He has also set eternity in the human heart'[9]—this might explain why we yearn for more than atoms and particles, more than just survival and reproduction."

As we continued to talk, he slowly opened up and revealed that he'd actually had a very strict religious background and in his twenties had rejected anything to do with God. "But for all of that," he admitted, "I do agree there are some things in life that probably don't really make sense without God."

One of the powerful things about *wondering* questions is that they work well with all age groups. Anybody can understand them if you ask them the right way. I have a friend who is a religious studies teacher in a high school in the south of England. As a Christian teaching in a secular school, he has to be very careful how direct he is about his faith, but John has found that asking

---

9 Ecclesiastes 3:11.

wondering questions can open up all kinds of conversations. On one occasion, he was teaching a class on ethics, and to illustrate a point about human rights, he put on the screen the cover of *Time Magazine* from August 9, 2010.[10]

That famous cover image shows the mutilated face of Bibi Aisha, a young Afghani girl who, after she ran away from a forced marriage to a Taliban warlord, had her nose and ears hacked off and was left to die in the mountains. She was rescued by aid workers and given reconstructive surgery. But it's a striking image, and as the class processed it, John asked, "Who here thinks that what was done to Bibi Aisha was wrong?"

Thankfully, every hand in the class went up (it's always a bad day for a teacher when you discover a psychopath lurking in class 5B). But John didn't stop there. He asked his teenage students, "Okay, but *why* is it wrong?"

There was a thoughtful silence before one student raised his hand and answered, "Because it's not right, Mr. Broadbanks, sir. It broke her human rights."

"Great answer, Kevin. But *why* is it wrong to violate a person's rights?"

"Well, it just *is*, sir."

"It just *is*?" replied John. "But have you wondered what's so magical about human rights? What's so special about possessing human DNA that means we automatically get granted value and dignity? Has anybody here ever wondered why?"

At the end of the ensuing discussion, John was able to say, "Do you know, when it comes to human rights, I wonder if we need to think really carefully about what we believe. If you believe

---

10 See Jodi Bieber, *Bibi Aisha*, July 15, 2010, photograph, *Time Magazine*, cover, August 2010, http://content.time .com/time/magazine/0,9263,7601100809,00.html.

in God, it is much easier to understand rights—God created us with value and dignity—than if you don't and think we are just a cosmic accident."

Not merely did this use of a *wondering* question lead to lots more conversations over the following weeks, it also opened up a conversation with his departmental head, who had been in the room observing the lesson. Later, in the staff room, this colleague (a self-described agnostic) remarked to John, "That was an absolutely fascinating discussion back there. It had never before occurred to me that human rights is a ludicrous idea if God doesn't exist. Maybe more things depend on belief in God than I'd considered."

Connecting the Little Story to the Big Story

I think one of the reasons that *wondering* questions work so well is we're starting from a place where somebody already *is*. Rather than thinking, *How can I browbeat my non-Christian friend into accepting a few basic Christian beliefs?* or worse, sitting there all depressed because your work colleagues don't show the slightest glimmer of any religious interest, you can use a *wondering* question and begin with the things they already care about. My friend Andy Kind, a very gifted comedian who came to faith in his twenties, puts it like this in his semi-autobiographical book, *Hidden in Plain Sight*:

> In my early twenties I didn't really know what I thought
> of the Big Story that the universe is telling. . . . There
> seemed to be an infinite number of religions, philosophies
> and conspiracy theories which sought to account for how
> and why the universe is as it is, and I wasn't sure which
> of those Big Stories out there was the real deal. But I did
> know something about my "Little Story." I knew that I

believed in Love. Not just love, but unconditional Love. I wanted to be loved without fear of rejection; loved for who I was and not based on what I did. . . . I believed in Justice. . . . I believed in Purpose. . . . I believed in Freedom. . . . I believed in Beauty. . . . I believed that death felt unnatural to observe, no matter how many times I observed it.[11]

For Andy, it was as friends helped him to *wonder* about these things that he began to realise it was only the Big Story of Christianity that made any sense of his Little Story. This is what *wondering* questions do so powerfully, as you:

- find something your friend is passionate about;
- take an interest in it—ask lots of questions and listen well;
- use a *wondering* question to gently introduce the idea that what they care about doesn't fit well in a godless world; and
- show that Christianity makes the best sense of it.

As C. S. Lewis, who himself came to faith through *wondering* questions and whose toolshed we briefly borrowed earlier, once wrote, "I believe in Christianity as I believe that the Sun has risen, not only because I see it, but because by it I see everything else."[12]

With practice, you can learn to ask *wondering* questions very easily, to "wonder out loud" as you discover the things that really matter to your friends and colleagues. By the way, one rich vein that you can mine for these kinds of questions is art like songs, novels, and movies. Most art raises fascinating questions that Christians

---

11 Andy Kind, *Hidden in Plain Sight: Clues You May Have Missed in the Search for Meaning* (Epsom, UK: Good Book Company, forthcoming), p.7.
12 C. S. Lewis, "Is Theology Poetry?" in *The Weight of Glory* (New York: HarperOne, 1980), 140.

can often use as gentle conversation starters. For example, I'm a massive Tolkien fan, probably because, being only 5'8", I've long felt an affinity with hobbits. But *The Lord of the Rings* (which is once again very topical, given Amazon's billion-dollar spin-off series) is brilliant for *wondering* questions: "I wonder why we love stories about good and evil?"; "I wonder why Tolkien portrayed evil as something that can corrupt even good people?"; "I wonder whether there's something in the idea that the ultimate salvation of the world comes not through power but through weakness and sacrifice?"

With a bit of thought, you can look for *wondering* questions in almost any film. After the most recent James Bond movie, *No Time to Die*,[13] I was able to start quite a few conversations by asking, "I wonder, is there *ever* a good time to die?"[14]

Wondering with Friends from Other Faiths

The great thing about *wondering* questions is they don't just work with agnostic or secular friends but can also be great conversation openers with friends from other faiths. In fact, there's a helpful example in the New Testament of Paul doing just this, which we looked at in chapter 5. In Acts 17, we find him in Athens, and as he tours the city, noticing all the statues, temples, and other pagan, polytheistic paraphernalia, Paul (as a good Jew) gets understandably distressed. But among all the assorted altars, Paul notices one with an intriguing inscription: "To an Unknown God." Later, when Paul has the chance to preach to an audience at the Areopagus, he effectively leads with a *wondering* question:

---

[13] Yes, I confess, I love the whole Bond franchise and like to imagine I bear a passing resemblance to Daniel Craig—if the lights are out and it's a moonless night.

[14] Here's a short newspaper article I wrote on this theme: "For Those Who Trust in Jesus, Tomorrow Never Dies," *The Scotsman*, October 21, 2021, https://www.scotsman.com/news/opinion/columnists/for-those-who-trust-in-jesus-tomorrow-never-dies-dr-andy-bannister-3426772.

> People of Athens! I see that in every way you are very
> religious. For as I walked around and looked carefully at
> your objects of worship, I even found an altar with this
> inscription: TO AN UNKNOWN GOD. So you are ignorant
> of the very thing you worship—and this is what I am
> going to proclaim to you.
>
> ACTS 17:22-23

In other words, Paul says, "I wonder if you've thought about
the *identity* of this unknown god to whom you've dedicated an
altar?"—and then goes on to tell the Athenians about the God
of the Bible (drawing, incidentally, from a few of the Greek poets
and writers his audience knew well). It's a brilliant example of how
to get an audience thinking about the gospel by starting from the
very things they're familiar with.

Over the years, I've had the privilege of participating in many
conversations with Muslim friends, students, or colleagues, and just
as Paul did in Athens, I've found *wondering* questions to be helpful.
For example, it may be the case that the Muslim I am chatting with,
on hearing me describe the God of the Bible as a "God of love," will
say something like "I also believe in a God of love." Now, the Qur'an
patently does *not* describe Allah this way,[15] but responding to my
Muslim friend with a sharp "No, you don't!" goes down about as
well as a cup of concrete coffee. Much better to ask some questions,
for instance, "I wonder why it is we're so drawn to the idea that God
is love?" or "I wonder, what's the greatest example of love you can
think of?" (And as we discuss that, I want to feed in what Jesus says
in John 15:13, that the greatest form of love is self-sacrifice.)

---

[15] For more detail on this, see Andy Bannister, *Do Muslims and Christians Worship the Same God?* (London: InterVarsity Press, 2021), 61–69, 156–160.

And as my Muslim friend and I talk about God and love, I'm looking and praying for the right moment when I can push in gently with words like "Do you know, the more you speak about God and love, the more it sounds like you are describing the God of the Bible rather than the God of the Qur'an. I wonder why that is?"

One of the beautiful things about the gospel is that Jesus fulfils all the hopes, desires, and longings that other faith traditions *promise* but fail to deliver on. People yearn for a God who truly loves them—this is only found in Christianity. Our Muslim friends proclaim, "Allahu Akbar!"—that God is great—but only in God's defeat of evil on the cross do we see true greatness. Our Buddhist friends yearn for an escape from the world of suffering; only Christianity talks realistically and honestly about suffering, offering real hope because the God of the Bible has not just *said* but *done* something about it. A good *wondering* question can help connect the religious longings of our friends to their true fulfilment in and through Jesus.

Following the Signposts

What we are aiming to do with a *wondering* question is what some have called "pre-evangelism," warming people up so they're ready for a spiritual conversation. Not least, people are not going to be interested in talking more deeply about Christianity if they don't think faith matters. But if we can show our friends, by means of *wondering* questions, that so much of what they care about—from justice to beauty, from purpose to identity—directly flows from what we think about God, that each of our personal "little stories" only makes sense if we are living in the right "big story," then fruitful conversations can follow. As the French Christian philosopher

Blaise Pascal so memorably put it, "Make [Christianity] attractive, make good men wish it were true, and then show that it is."[16]

But with a *wondering* question, we're not just gently prompting our friends to ponder how the things they care most about are only possible if God is real. We're also encouraging them to consider things like hope, love, meaning, purpose, beauty, and so forth as *signposts*. The thing about a signpost is we don't just want people to stop and admire it—"What a lovely signpost! Look at the way the light strikes it, the beautiful font they've used. Of all the signposts I've ever seen, that is by far the prettiest. Let's stop and have our picnic here." No, the *point* of a signpost is to follow it to where it's pointing.

So if *wondering* questions are great at highlighting the signposts, how do we encourage our friends to follow and walk further along the road? That's where our fourth question, the *whether* question, is going to be really helpful.

---

16 Blaise Pascal, Penseés, III.187.

CHAPTER 11

THE *WHETHER* QUESTION

IMAGINE THE SCENE: IT'S CHRISTMAS DAY, and so far, everything has gone swimmingly. Last night it snowed, so it's a white Christmas (although the cat got buried under a snow drift). The carols have been sung, the turkey dinner cooked and eaten, the crackers pulled, and the brandy bottle rescued from the clutches of Uncle Jim. Now, the whole family is gathered around the tree as the presents are distributed. The final gift to be passed out is a large, beautifully wrapped box from your best buddy, and you eagerly rip off the paper to discover not one but *three* gifts. Your friend has bought you a set of bathroom scales, a bulk box of super strong deodorant (branded "Let's KO that BO!"), and a book bearing the title *How to Be Less of an Annoying Twerp*. (They have even premarked helpful passages with Post-it Notes.)

Thankfully, this is just a thought experiment. But I imagine that were such a thing to actually occur, your so-called best friend's choice of gifts would probably go down like a lead hippo. Indeed, I suspect your friendship would soon be hippo-posthumous.

The fact is, we don't like to be told uncomfortable truths directly—and certainly not publicly—especially if the truths being shared directly challenge our status, our identity, or our most deeply held beliefs or worldview. And this is where the bicycle of evangelism can sometimes run into the treacle puddle of objection, because what we are telling our non-Christian friends cuts so radically counter to what they believe.

Whether it's the lifestyle changes that your friend thinks might follow if Christianity is true or simply that they have been told since they were knee-high to a grasshopper that the world is secular, that there is no God, and that if you can't touch, taste, or stub your toe on it in the dark, it doesn't exist—there is a huge gap between what they believe and what you want to tell them. It's going to take more than a trampoline and a pair of cardboard wings to get you across the chasm of plausibility.

And this is where the *whether* question can prove helpful. To once again borrow a metaphor from C. S. Lewis, "watchful dragons" often guard the front doors of people's minds, but maybe there is a way to tiptoe quietly past them with a carefully worded question.

Come and See

The *whether* question works by inviting your friend to consider whether it is possible that Christianity could be true, whether it might offer a helpful, even compelling, angle on a question or shed more light on their situation. With a *whether* question you're inviting your friend to "come and see" what Jesus might have to say about the situation. Let's consider an example of the *whether* question in action.

My friend Matt is a counsellor and works as part of a team of therapists in a small counselling practice in the outskirts of London. On one occasion, Matt was having a beer with Steve, one of his colleagues. They got on well, and in previous conversations, faith issues had often risen to the surface like croutons in an onion soup. Every time, though, Steve would then veer the conversation away somewhere else. But this time, whilst they were talking, Steve mentioned how earlier that day he had been counselling a client struggling with issues of self-worth. "His life is a *real* mess," Steve said sadly. "Fired from his job, wife left him, and the house is about to be repossessed. I can partly understand why he feels life isn't worth living."

"That's really tough," agreed Matt. "So what *do* you say to someone whose life is, on every conceivable metric, worthless and pointless? Job gone, wife gone, taking the kids with her—"

"Or leaving them, if they're teenagers," chipped in Steve.

"Good point. Maybe they've also got no friends at all, have recently received a terrible health diagnosis, and the dog's just died. There's literally not a glimmer of hope to be found. So, what do you say when someone comes to you struggling with their self-image?"

Steve thought for a while, swilling the dregs of his pint of Fiddler's Elbow around the glass. Finally, he said, "I guess we have to tell them the noble lie, right?"

"The noble lie?"

"You know—we tell them they are worth it, that they're special and valued and so on."

"Even if you don't believe it?" asked Matt.

"Yeah, it feels totally fraudulent," admitted Steve. "But what else can you do?"

Because they'd spoken about spirituality before, even if Steve had rarely wanted to talk about it for long, Matt felt the opportunity was right to try again. "I hope you don't mind my saying, but this is one of many reasons why I'm a Christian."

"Why? What's religion got to do with it?"

"Well, I wonder *whether* you've considered that *if* Christianity *is* true, that would arguably give a terrifically secure grounding for our identity and self-worth? After all, the Bible says we were made in God's image, and God showed how he values us by sending Jesus to give his life for us. None of that guarantees life will be full of roses and kittens—"

"I've got a fur allergy anyway," Steve replied, grinning.

"—but it would mean that our value depends not on circumstances but on something far more concrete. And we wouldn't need to lie to our patients. What do you think?"

No weeping repentance immediately followed, but the conversation did open up into, as Matt described it, "the most productive discussion about spiritual things I've had in five years of working with Steve." And the turning point was that *whether* question. Matt hadn't insisted, "You *must* believe this!" but had encouraged his colleague to consider whether some not insignificant things changed if Christianity is true.

In this case, Matt was dealing with somebody who wasn't hostile to Christianity but who just hadn't wanted to "go there" in previous conversations. But the beauty of a *whether* question is you can use it also with friends who are more overtly sceptical. For example, I was talking on one occasion to a student who made a fairly typical atheist remark about Christianity, words to the effect of "I'm amazed anyone can believe in things like miracles. We don't need God; we live in an age of science."

Now, there are lots of things that could be said by way of response to this, but I thought I'd try a *whether* question: "I love science too. But I wonder *whether* you've overstated things here a bit? After all, science has its miracles too, I think."

"Such as?"

"How do you think the universe began?"

"The big bang, obviously."

"Yes, but before that?"

"Well—" the student shifted uneasily in her seat—"I guess things just came from nothing, right?"

"That's a common view. Indeed, the atheist physicist Lawrence Krauss even wrote a book called *A Universe from Nothing*."

The student looked relieved to be in good company. "Ah. That's okay then."

"Well, it *isn't* really, is it? Have you ever considered *whether* what you now have is a choice? Roll up, roll up, ladies and gentlemen, and pick your miracle—on the left, we have God, creating the universe and all that exists; on the right, we have, well, nothing making everything. Have you considered *whether* it's you, my friend, who has the bigger miracle at this point to explain?"

Again, although I did it in that slightly cheeky way which we Brits specialise in,[1] I was using exactly the same approach Matt had with his colleague. Rather than push back directly with a rebuttal, what I did was invite the student to consider whether there was a different way of seeing things.

---

[1] And that has produced great comedy as well as many international diplomatic incidents.

Using a *Whether* Question with Agnostic Friends

Another setting where a *whether* question can prove helpful is when talking with friends who are agnostic. If you recall, an agnostic is somebody who, when it comes to spiritual matters, is at the place on the map marked "I don't know."

A few years ago, a friend and I were on a fishing trip on Loch Tay, a beautiful stretch of water an hour's drive from where I lived in Scotland. Neither of us had a boat, so we had hired a fishing guide to take us out. As the little wooden craft putt-putt-puttered its way along the loch, the guide began making conversation and quickly discovered that my friend was a pastor and that I spent my time telling people about Jesus. "Och, so I've two religious types with me today, have I then?" He muttered something under his breath in Gaelic, which I suspect translated to "What did I do to deserve this?"

"So what do you believe about God?" my friend asked.

Our fishing guide shrugged. "I don't really know. It's not that I don't believe in God, it's not that I do. I canna say. How can we know, eh?"

"Fair enough," my friend said. "You know, there's a fancy name for what you said: agnosticism. It's a posh way of saying, 'I'm not sure.'"

"Aye, that'd be right."

It was now my turn to say something, and I used a *whether* question:[2] "But I wonder *whether* you've considered that there are two types of agnostics—"

"Two types?"

"Yes. You can be an agnostic because you really want to know but you haven't yet found out—or because you simply can't be

---

[2] When on a Scottish loch in October, always think about the weather.

bothered (or are too afraid) to learn. You can be an open-minded agnostic or a lazy agnostic. Have you ever thought *whether* one of those better describes where you're at?"

"You're saying I'm lazy?"

"No, no," I said hastily, remembering the old proverb "Whoever annoys the boatman had better be able to swim." "I just wondered *whether* you'd realised that those were the two options?"

The boatman stroked his beard thoughtfully. "Aye, well I guess whether there's a God or not is probably something one ought to know . . ."

"A bit like 'Did I put the plug in the bottom of the boat?'" chipped in my friend.

"Aye. But look, my old mum used to drag my brothers and me along to church when we were kids. None of it really went in, if I'm honest."

"Where did you grow up?" my friend asked.

"Aberfeldy, a few miles up the road."

"I visited there for the first time yesterday," I said. "For years I've driven through it on the way to somewhere else. I must have been *through* it dozens of times. Yesterday, for the first time ever, I spent some time there, explored the town. I wonder *whether* something similar sometimes happens with Christianity. It's easy to whizz through it—like you did in your childhood—but never really stop and look at it properly."

"I see what you're angling at," the fishing guide said. "So how would one do that?"

Now *there* was a question.

Another approach I have sometimes used with friends who play the "I don't know" card when it comes to spiritual things is to ask a question like this: "I wonder *whether* you've ever thought

about the huge weight of evidence in favour of Christianity?"
Now, sometimes this will get you nowhere, in which case you
move on. On other occasions, I've had friends respond, "Evidence?
What kind of evidence?"—for in many people's minds the words
religion and *evidence* go together as naturally as the words *exciting* and *soup*. What should you say by way of reply if your friend
responds this way? I tend to offer four pieces of evidence, usually
in this order:

1. The fact that anything at all exists
2. The fact that the laws of nature are so beautifully balanced
   or "fine-tuned" for life
3. The fact that we seem to live in a moral universe, where
   good and evil aren't just personal preferences
4. The fact that the life, death, and resurrection of Jesus
   stand up to historical scrutiny

If you're new to some of those arguments, you'll find a helpful
list of resources in appendix 2 (see page 251), with recommended
books and websites suitable for all levels.

A Brief Word about Evidence

At this point it is probably worth saying a brief word about evidence, as there is a great deal of confusion about the word. Despite
the noisy protestations of some celebrity atheists—and the over-
enthusiastic preaching of some celebrity evangelists—when it
comes to spiritual questions, there are no 100 percent water-
tight, totally knockdown arguments for or against the truth of
the Christian faith. It may surprise you to hear me say that,[3] but

---

3 "Isn't Bannister a Christian apologist?" "Yes, but he is British." "Ah, that explains it!"

then this is actually true of almost anything in the world. Apart, possibly, from very specialised fields such as mathematics, where we can *prove* that 2 + 2 = 4,[4] in the real world, most of the time, there may be a pile of evidence in favour of something, but there is also always a gap of uncertainty. You can't *prove* the chair is strong enough to sit on, or that the plane won't fall out of the sky, or that your eyes aren't deceiving you, or that Caesar crossed the Rubicon, or that the word should definitely be pronounced "tomato." Instead, in the real world, what we're interested in is how *strong* the evidence is in favour of what we are proposing to do or believe.

So in a conversation, when somebody asks about the *evidence* for Christianity, I usually find it helpful to reply with a *whether* question: "I wonder *whether* you've thought about the *kind* of evidence that would be persuasive?" And if I get the chance, I'll aim to follow up by saying, "I wonder *whether* it would be more helpful if God had given not just one showy piece of evidence but lots of different pieces, which taken together might be really compelling?" Indeed, *weight* of evidence is what we look for in so many other areas of life—and we then ask what best fits with that pile of evidence. For example, I walk into the kitchen and see a chair has been moved below a high cupboard, the cookie jar raided, crumbs scattered all over the floor, and sticky finger marks left on the countertop. All this fits really well with the theory that one of the smaller members of the household has taken my joke about sugar being a food group too literally. Or imagine that when NASA astronauts landed on the moon in 1969, they'd found a series of strange footprints, a metal tablet with an unknown language

---

4 Although I once used this illustration in a talk and had a lecturer in mathematics accost me afterwards and point out that before we possibly say 2 + 2 = 4, we first need to decide what we mean by concepts like *2, 4, +,* and = (and possibly words like *obsessive*).

engraved on it, and marks left in the ground from the landing gear of some kind of spaceship. Although Neil Armstrong would not have met ET in person, there is still a very powerful argument that "aliens made it to the moon first" fits better with the data than alternative theories, such as "the Russians snuck in overnight and borrowed the sound stage to shoot their fake moon landing first."

Of all the arguments I've heard for Christianity over the years (and there are some excellent ones), I am still of the view that the most *powerful* is this claim that Christianity makes the best sense of dozens of pieces of evidence—whether it's the longings and desires we talked about in the last chapter, or whether it's the origins of the universe, morality, and the historical life, death, and resurrection of Jesus. A *whether* question is a helpful way to introduce this big idea into conversations with friends.

Using the Four Questions Together

Just as the many pieces of evidence for Christianity are far more compelling when weighed together, so the four questions we have looked at—*what, why, wondering,* and *whether*—are likewise especially effective when they're combined.

I have a Canadian friend who frequently has to fly extensively for work, and over the years he has practised ways to start spiritual conversations with other passengers. John will often begin by making small talk with the person seated next to him—this breaks the ice a bit (and John can discern if this is somebody happy to chat or if they'd prefer to jam their earbuds in or spend the flight with their nose in a paperback copy of *Beekeeping for Dummies*[5]). If they're open to conversation, John will ask them lots of friendly questions—about their reason for flying, their job, their family,

---

[5] I paid £20 for that book; I clearly got stung.

and so on. And then at the right moment, he'll ask, "So are you happy?" Whatever the answer, John will then introduce a *what* question into the conversation: "Happiness seems to be such an overused word in our culture, doesn't it? *What* do you think the word *happiness* actually means?"

He'll listen to their answer, and when they're done, John will follow up with "Did you know that the ancient thinkers, chaps like Plato and Aristotle and that bunch, thought there were actually *four* levels of happiness and that we can only be truly, ultimately happy in life if we find happiness at all four levels?"

The clever thing about this is that people *love* lists. Think of how many online articles reel you in with headlines like "10 Cures for Halitosis" or "23 Garlic Recipes to Surprise Your Loved Ones." It's very hard when somebody says, "There are four types of happiness" to avoid scratching the itch of curiosity and asking, "Really?"

John will then explain that happiness level 1 is animal happiness and is basically about the fulfilment of appetite. "I am hungry. My tummy is rumbling. I see the donut, I eat the donut, it makes me feel good, and I am happy. I can repeat this a few times until I am full." It's easy, but it's transient; it's quickly over.

The problem, however, is that when we misuse our appetites, we don't get happiness; we get unhappiness. For example, if we misuse food to cope with anxiety and depression, we can end up with what doctors call an eating disorder. Similarly, our culture is increasingly telling us we can treat sex like food—if we feel like it, sleep with somebody. But the problem is that if we have sex unconnected from committed love, it often becomes first boring and then perverted, producing not happiness but unhappiness. That's why so many people have transient relationships—they're trying to use sex to fill the gap that love is supposed to fill. It quickly becomes boring, and they move on to the next relationship.

The only escape from unhappiness level 1 is to move up to happiness level 2. John will then wait politely and expectantly, because he ideally wants his new friend to ask, "So what's happiness level 2?"

"I'm glad you asked!" John will say, before explaining that happiness level 2 is all about comparison. "I have more of something than the next person. I have more money, more influence, greater success." Some have called this "the comparison game," and there's nothing necessarily wrong with this—with developing a skill and doing it well. Excelling in a sport, succeeding at work, or doing well in business can bring great happiness. But the problem is that if we try to live our life at this level, it produces not happiness but unhappiness, largely because it's so stressful. We're constantly faced with nagging questions: *What happens when I am no longer at the top? What happens if I make a mistake and am fired? What happens if my performance metrics begin to fall or if my company hires a new employee who is better than me?* Very soon we find ourselves in unhappiness level 2, from which the only way out is to move up to happiness level 3.

"Yeah, I kind of get that. So what's happiness level 3?"

"Excellent question!" John will say. He'll then go on to say that happiness level 3 comes through living for somebody other than ourselves, investing entirely in doing something for others. It's liberating and wonderful, primarily because it's not competitive. Perhaps the best example is parenthood. But even those who aren't parents can still find happiness level 3 through serving others, through giving their time, effort, or resources to help others.

But there's a problem with happiness level 3. The problem

is it comes to an end. Children soon grow up and leave home. People we've invested in will eventually move on and no longer need us. We cannot be everything to somebody else, and if we try, we will end up in unhappiness level 3. Furthermore, there's also a risk that happiness level 3 is actually profoundly selfish—the *real* reason we're helping others is to make ourselves feel better. In which case, we're not helping *them*, we're helping *ourselves*. The only way out of this mess is to move up to the final level, happiness level 4.

"Okay, so what's happiness level 4?"

Before answering that, this is where John—who started this discussion with a *what* question—will often use a *why* question: "Before I answer that, *why* do you think it matters that we find a basis for happiness that can truly sustain us?" There's also a very easy *wondering* question in here too: "I *wonder* why it is that human beings are the only animal that needs more than food, sex, and competition to sustain us?" John will talk about this with them for a while, occasionally dropping in little references to happiness level 4. Finally, after being asked a few times, "So what *is* level 4?" John likes to respond by saying with a twinkle in his eye, "I'm afraid I can't tell you."

"What do you mean, you *can't* tell me?"

"Well, this has been a great conversation, and—well, sometimes level 4 annoys people."

"But you can't just leave it hanging!"

"Okay, well, just remember that you insisted . . ." And then John will share his testimony, explaining how he tried to find happiness, peace, security, and identity in the first three levels but found they let him down miserably before finally he discovered that what he was most deeply looking for was what Jesus offered when he promised, "I have come that they may have life, and have it to the full."[6] John will end by saying, "I'm not saying you need to believe what I believe. But I *am* saying that unless you find something *like* that, you will never be truly and ultimately happy. I wonder *whether* you've discovered something like this yet?"

John has had thousands of these conversations over the years, and in many cases the conversation ends up going much deeper. He has had the privilege of talking easily about Jesus with people from all walks of life and has even on a few occasions been able to pray with them to become Christians right there on the plane.[7]

As I think about how John bridged the conversation to Jesus with that final *whether* question, it strikes me that Jesus' entire ministry was designed to generate *whether* questions. Think, for example, of that famous scene at the end of John 1:

The next day Jesus decided to leave for Galilee. Finding Philip, he said to him, "Follow me."

Philip, like Andrew and Peter, was from the town of Bethsaida. Philip found Nathanael and told him, "We have found the one Moses wrote about in the Law, and about whom the prophets also wrote—Jesus of Nazareth, the son of Joseph."

"Nazareth! Can anything good come from there?" Nathanael asked.

"Come and see," said Philip.

JOHN 1:43-46

---

6 John 10:10.

7 You can find a lot of other material by John at www.johnpatrick.ca. His "Four Levels of Happiness" approach is based in part on Robert J. Spitzer, *Ten Universal Principles: A Brief Philosophy of the Life Issues* (San Francisco: Ignatius Press, 2011), 91–101.

Although Nathanael is a sceptic (not least because he's a bit of a snob and considers Nazareth to be a one-camel town full of rednecks and hillbillies), he is nevertheless intrigued enough by Philip's question ("I wonder *whether* this could be the Messiah!") that when Philip follows up with "Come and see," Nathanael is willing to go and meet Jesus. And as you read the Gospels, you see this pattern time and time again. "Who *is* Jesus?" ask the disciples, the crowds, the authorities: "I wonder *whether* he might be who he claims to be?"

And this is what we're aiming to do in our conversations with our friends, neighbours, and coworkers. Not to be clever or smug, not to try to win arguments or to show off, but through asking good questions, listening well, and creating space for spiritual conversations, we want to find the opportunity to invite people to consider *whether*, to "Come and see!"

But what if after all of this—after we've carefully used the *what, why, wondering,* and *whether* questions and listened and engaged well—what if after all that, our friends still have serious objections, challenges, or questions for us? In the next chapter I'll share with you an easy-to-learn five-step (remember what I said about lists!) approach you can use when it's time to stop asking questions and to start offering answers.

CHAPTER 12

FIVE SIMPLE STEPS FOR ANSWERING TOUGH QUESTIONS

WE ARE NATURALLY SUSPICIOUS OF people who repeatedly duck difficult questions—or at least we should be. I learnt this the hard way when I bought my first car. I had just turned twenty, was young, fresh-faced, and naive, and I didn't spot the warning signs when I innocently asked, "So exactly how many miles has this vehicle done?"

Mr. Dibbler, our local car dealer, patted the roof of the little Ford. "They don't make 'em like this anymore," he said, puffing on an enormous cigar. "This colour was discontinued. What you are looking at here is positively vintage, a rare collector's item."

"Sure, but how many miles has it done?"

"And it's been looked after beautifully," the dealer continued. "One careful elderly lady owner, who cared for it like it was a beloved pet. Rarely drove it, too, so the interior's like pressed iron."

"You mean pristine?"

"That too."

"But what's the mileage?"

"Look, son," said the dealer, putting an arm around my shoulder and smiling in the friendly, toothy way that a barracuda might at a passing herring, "I ought to charge you £1,000 for this beauty—but tell you what, she can be yours for £600, and that's cutting me own throat."

Several months and many repair bills later, as I sat in the smoking remains of the car after the engine had blown itself to pieces in the middle of one of the busiest intersections in London, I reflected that maybe I should not have bought a rusty bucket of bolts from a man who refused to answer a question, even if the British racing-green-with-orange-go-faster-stripes paint job did look particularly natty.

Whether it's car dealers who refuse to tell you the mileage, politicians saying, "That's a stupid question" when journalists ask a perfectly proper one, or small children who when asked, "Have you cleaned your room?" point out the window and say, "Look, Dad, a squirrel!" we should indeed be very suspicious if somebody flat-out refuses to answer a question.

Sadly, the church sometimes has a bit of a reputation for being a place where questions are not welcome. I was once chatting with a University of Toronto student, who said, with a note of sadness in his voice, "I used to be a Christian, but I'm not any longer."

"What happened?" I asked.

"It's simple, really. I was raised in a very, very fundamentalist church, but in my teens, I discovered a love for science. So when it was time for university, I came here to the University of Toronto to study biology. Quickly it became obvious there were massive contradictions between what I was being taught at university and what my church had taught me about origins—the book of Genesis, that kind of stuff. So I made an appointment to see my pastor and ask for his help."

"Great idea," I said. "There are some brilliant books and resources on that question. Did your pastor direct you to some that could help?"

"Not exactly."

"Oh? What did he say?"

"He was dismissive," the student said, his voice now angrier. "*Totally* dismissive. He looked at me and said, 'Oh, it's really easy, son, really easy: you choose the Bible or you choose biology. Next question, please.'"

"So what did you do?"

"Simple. I chose biology."

I confess that conversation moved me almost to tears. For whilst I was thankfully able to introduce the student to some useful resources written by Christians in the sciences, a tremendous amount of damage had been done because his clueless pastor had dismissed his perfectly valid question. He hadn't asked a question back. He hadn't engaged the young man in dialogue. He hadn't offered any help. And in so doing, he'd convinced the student that Christianity *had* no answers.

As we speak with our friends, neighbours, and colleagues, it is essential that if they have questions or objections to our faith, we do our very best to address them. For sure, we want to begin with the *what, why, wondering,* and *whether* questions—these can be tremendously helpful in exploring ideas or turning a challenge into a conversation. But whilst we want to *begin* with questions, we don't want to stay there. Prawn cocktail, garlic bread, or poppadoms and mango chutney may make brilliant starters,[1] but there's a time to move on from the starter to the main course. Similarly, whilst questions can help us start (or stay in) a conversation, if our friends have substantive questions of their own, we need to address them. Otherwise we risk people assuming that there are no answers to be found.

Answering Tough Questions: Some Practical Basics

So how do we go about answering a friend who has a difficult question, an objection, or a stumbling block that prevents them from progressing further on their spiritual journey? Well, let's begin with four simple principles.

First, remember that our task is to answer the *questioner*, not the question. Behind every question, behind every objection to the gospel is an individual person, and that's who we want to reach. If as I'd spoken with the student at the University of Toronto I'd simply thought, *This is the "God and Science Question;" let me download answer #42 from my answer bank*, I'd have missed something important.

Second, remember to clarify a question or objection using your *what* and *why* questions. For example, when I meet somebody who has a question or objection to Christianity, a really helpful early response is something like "That's a really interesting question. Tell me, *why* do you ask it?" For example, if your friend is asking how you can be a Christian and believe in an all-powerful, all-good God given the existence of suffering in the world, it is probably helpful to discover that the reason they're asking this is not because they want an abstract philosophical

---

[1] Although not eaten simultaneously.

discussion but because their best friend has just been diagnosed with terminal cancer.

Third, be willing to admit your limitations. If your friend has asked you a question that you feel confident addressing, brilliant. But if you only have a few crumbs of wisdom to share, be open about that. You might say, "You know, that's a fantastic question, and I'm not a great thinker, just somebody who does their best to follow Jesus. But let me share a couple of things that might be helpful." And if all else fails, don't be afraid to confess total ignorance—but to offer to find the answer for them. (There is one crucial caveat to this. Be aware that there are questions which every Christian really needs to have thought about. For example, should your friend ask how you can believe in God given all the pain and suffering in the world and you reply, "Do you know, I've no idea! I've never thought about that before!" your friend probably isn't going to be impressed by your humility but stunned by your naivete. "What do you mean, you've never thought about pain and suffering before? Where on earth have you been living?")

That observation leads to our fourth practical principle—namely, the advice we read in 1 Peter 3:15 to "always be prepared." How can we put this into practice? Well, what are the questions and issues your friends are concerned with? What are the kinds of questions about Christianity that you've heard before or that are circulating in the culture? What can you read, watch, or listen to that could equip you with some helpful things to say in response?

Learning to SHARE an Answer

With those basic principles in place, how then do we respond to a friend who has a tough question or challenging objection to the gospel? From lots of practice over the years, as well as having learnt so much from watching others who do this well, I think there are five helpful steps to go through when answering a question about Christianity. And to make them easy to remember, I've created an acronym around the word *SHARE*,[2] which works like this.

First, we have S, for *sympathise*. When somebody asks a question about our faith, we want to begin by making a connection, by affirming the questioner, perhaps by acknowledging that we had that question ourselves in the past. Even something as simple as saying "That's a great question" can build rapport with the person we are talking with.

Next up is H, for *hidden assumptions*. Behind every question there is often a barrel load of assumptions, lurking unnoticed below the surface like an iceberg in a shipping lane. Before we offer a Christian perspective on the question our friend has raised, it's important that we draw their attention to things they may not have considered in their own beliefs. Trusty *what* and *why* questions can help bring assumptions to the surface.

Third, we come to A, for *apply the Bible*. In answering a friend's question, we want to invite them to explore the question from the perspective of the gospel—because where you look at things *from* can change your view entirely. In the sixth of his Narnia novels, *The Silver Chair*, there's a series of events where C. S. Lewis cleverly plays with this idea of perspective. The story's heroes—the children Eustace and Jill and the Marsh-wiggle Puddleglum—are crossing the wild wastelands of Ettinsmoor on a night of wild weather. The wind is blowing a gale, the snow is drifting, and they're half-frozen to death, when

---

[2] Some of the ideas in this section had their birth in a talk that Glen Scrivener and I jointly gave at the Premier Unbelievable Conference in London in 2018.

suddenly [Jill] skidded, slid about five feet, and found herself to her horror sliding down into a dark, narrow chasm which seemed that moment to have appeared in front of her. Half a second later she had reached the bottom. She appeared to be in a kind of trench or groove, only about three feet wide. And though she was shaken by the fall, almost the first thing she noticed was the relief of being out of the wind; for the walls of the trench rose high above her.[3]

Climbing down carefully, Eustace and Puddleglum join Jill and quickly discover this is not just one trench but a maze of twisty little passages, all alike. Finally, they escape the labyrinth and make their way to the nearby giant's castle of Harfang, from which, as they gaze out of a window the next morning, they see that the trenches in which they were blundering around were actually an inscription: the words "UNDER ME" carved in gigantic letters cut deep into the very granite of the hillside. This was a vital clue to their quest that at the start of the story they had been expressly told to look out for, yet they'd missed it because their viewpoint was wrong.

Likewise, when it comes to the questions or difficulties about faith that our friends want to ask about, something similar can be going on. From ground level, they can sometimes look unanswerable; but walk up the hill to the foot of the Cross and consider the question from there, and they can appear quite different.

Next, we come to R, for *retell the gospel story*. This is a crucial step. We don't simply want to give an intellectually wise or even

---

3 C. S. Lewis, *The Silver Chair* (London: HarperCollins, 2015), 80.

pastorally sensitive answer to our friend's question *and leave it there*—we want our friend to see Jesus more clearly. And so, as we engage with their question, it can be helpful to be thinking to ourselves, *How do I explain something of the gospel through this question?*

Fifth and finally, we have E, for *equip your friend*. If the question your friend has asked is complex or sensitive, it's likely that in a brief answer you will only be able to be, well, brief. So try where you can to direct them to a resource that can take them further on their spiritual journey—perhaps a video or podcast, a book or article, that they can engage with later. (By the way, if you're thinking to yourself, *But how do I know what resources to recommend?* then in appendix 2 at the back of the book you'll find a list of helpful resources both for equipping yourself and for recommending to others.)

Those are the five steps that I try to use whenever I'm faced with a tough question from a friend, neighbour, or colleague, and I hope the SHARE acronym makes them easy to remember.[4]

"But what do these five steps look like in practice?" I hear you cry. That's a great question—so let's take a look. What follows are three short examples. We'll consider the questions of suffering, of some of the violent passages in the Old Testament, and of the uniqueness of Jesus in a world of other faiths, and briefly see how we could use the SHARE approach in addressing them.

Example #1: Pain and Suffering

One of the most common questions I hear about Christianity concerns the issue of evil and suffering. "How can you be a Christian,"

---

[4] Acronyms are not my strong point, and it took me hours to come up with this one. I had thought that my first attempt, QWKZE, displayed real potential, but then an Eastern European friend told me that in her language *qwkze* means "a small, salted pork sausage traditionally given to a great aunt at Christmas," which I thought might prove a distraction for some readers.

someone may ask, "given the messy, broken, hurting world we find ourselves in?" Sometimes the question comes in a sharper, more personal form: "If God is good, why did my friend get attacked or my sister die of cancer?" Let's think about how we might offer an answer using the SHARE method I outlined above. Because of limited space, I'll offer just a few thoughts of what I might say under each step, but in a real-world conversation you would want to go slower and more carefully, not least when the topic, like this one, is potentially so pastorally sensitive.

Sympathise

I begin by thanking the person for their question and, if they talked about their personal experience of pain or injustice, thanking them for their honesty. I will often add that this is an issue I've personally thought about and wrestled with over the years, not least when evil or suffering has struck close to home. A family friend of ours was once attacked in the street on his way home from work and beaten up so violently, he was never able to work again. Ten years ago, when first trying to start a family, we experienced several miscarriages, and the pain of failed pregnancy after failed pregnancy caused us to struggle with this question in a deeply personal way.

Hidden Assumptions

But of course it's not just Christians who need to wrestle with the question of suffering and evil. Atheists have some questions to answer too. For example, why does evil or injustice or pain seem so wrong? After all, if humans are just a random assortment of atoms, why does it matter what happens to them? Furthermore, where do we get the idea that suffering and death aren't right? And once we start throwing around labels like "good" and "evil," what do we mean by them? Aren't those words just personal preferences in a godless universe? I wonder whether Christianity, although it has some questions to answer here, gives us a far better framework for speaking of "good" and "evil." As C. S. Lewis, who was an atheist for almost half of his life, wrote, "My argument against God was that the universe seemed so cruel and unjust. But how had I got this idea of *just* and *unjust*? A man does not call a line crooked unless he has some idea of a straight line."[5]

Apply the Bible

One of the things I find so helpful about Christianity is that the Bible is refreshingly honest about evil and suffering and on its very first page talks about the fact that the world is not the way God intended it to be. Rather, something has gone radically wrong with his good creation, caused by human beings trying to throw him out of the picture and make themselves the centre of the story.

But the Bible is also clear that pain and suffering, evil and death will not have the last word. For the Bible tells the much bigger story of God's plan to restore and renew his creation and to destroy evil once and for all. I wonder whether, when we naturally react with horror at suffering or death or injustice, we're actually revealing that instinctively, in the very deepest fibre of our being, that we know the Bible's take on evil and suffering is true.

---

5 C. S. Lewis, *Mere Christianity* (Glasgow: Collins, 1990), 31.

Retell the Gospel

Have you ever wondered that what most of us want when it comes to evil and suffering is not something *said* about it but something *done* about it? Indeed, we admire those who dedicate their lives to alleviating suffering, who demonstrate compassion.

Compassion is a fascinating word. Composed of two Latin words—*com* (meaning "with") and *passio* (meaning "suffer")—compassion literally means "to suffer alongside." In other words, *compassion* means to do something about suffering at such cost to yourself that you literally suffer too.

At the heart of the Christian faith is a God who hasn't just *said* something about suffering but who, in the cross of Jesus Christ, has *done* something about evil and suffering, defeating and disarming it at Calvary. But that defeat came at a great price. We see in Jesus a God of compassion, a God who does not merely give us the ability to name evil for what it is but a God who dealt with it and has given us the certain hope that one day evil will be gone forever.

Equip Your Friend

There is much more that could be said (and your friend may have many questions as you share some of the above). This is an area where I find it especially helpful to be aware of good resources, especially books that I can give to those who are struggling personally with suffering. Three that are particularly helpful are Sharon Dirckx's book *Why?: Looking At God, Evil and Personal Suffering*, Amy Orr-Ewing's *Where Is God in All the Suffering?* and Jeremy Marshall's *Beyond the Big C: Hope in the Face of Death*. All three authors come at the question of God and suffering from both a biblical and a very personal perspective.

Example #2: Violence in the Old Testament

A second objection I have encountered over the years concerns the violent passages in the Old Testament: "How can you believe in a God of love when he commands the Israelites to kill the Canaanites?" An atheist friend once put it even more bluntly: "Doesn't the God of the Bible have a split personality: judgement in the Old Testament, love in the New Testament?"

Sympathise

Whenever I'm asked this question, I always begin by acknowledging that the questioner has a point. There are many passages in the Old Testament, not least in the book of Joshua, which, when I read them, I think, *Gosh!*[6] If we haven't wondered how all of this fits with Jesus' command to "lay down your sword" and "love your enemies," perhaps we haven't read carefully enough. So acknowledge the question—because it's a good one!

Hidden Assumptions

At the same time, I would want to ask my friend some questions as we explore this topic. For example, "Have you ever wondered if there are occasions when violence *is* permitted? What would those situations be?" If they are deeply committed to pacifism, we might ask why—where precisely does the idea that love is the supreme value come from? Again, if we live in a purely materialistic universe, where natural selection is the only game in town, isn't the

---

[6] We Brits are masters of understatement.

triumph of the strong over the weak all that matters? I wonder whether the very fact that we read the Old Testament and think, *Ouch!* is a sign of how deeply Jesus' values and ethics have seeped into our culture, no matter how secular we like to think we are.

Apply the Bible

I will sometimes say to friends who ask this question, "Did you know that the problem of God's love and God's judgement is actually raised by the Bible itself?" One of the oldest books of the Old Testament is Jonah, and in it there's an amazing moment where Jonah has a massive whinge about God's character. God had sent him to preach to Jonah's sworn enemies, the Assyrians, who proceeded to repent of their evil, and God then holds back from destroying them. This drives Jonah nuts, and he yells at God,

> Isn't this what I said, LORD, when I was still at home?
> That is what I tried to forestall by fleeing to Tarshish.
> I knew that you are a gracious and compassionate God,
> slow to anger and abounding in love, a God who relents
> from sending calamity. Now, LORD, take away my life,
> for it is better for me to die than to live.
>
> JONAH 4:2-3

In other words, Jonah thinks God—the *Old Testament God*—is too loving, too merciful, and too compassionate. What Jonah was struggling with was God's *love* and God's *judgement*. But the Bible doesn't see these things as contradictory—rather, God's judgement *flows out of* his love. Judgement is not the opposite of love; rather, if I truly love somebody, I will care deeply if they are wronged or oppressed. And that, says the Bible, is one of the reasons God acts in this way—he loves the world he has made, and when he sees injustice, evil, and violence, God will bring judgement.

Coming back to the book of Joshua, we see something similar at play. The Israelites were not asked to destroy a nation of vegan, kitten-hugging, pacifist knitting enthusiasts. Rather, from what we know of Canaanite society, it was truly evil—one in which, for example, children would be burnt alive in the worship of the god Molech. But nor does God rush to judgement—earlier in the Old Testament he says to Abraham that he will grant the Canaanites four hundred years, but then the time will come for judgement.[7]

What I'm aiming to do here is to help my friend to see the wider story, because context is crucial. Imagine you have never seen the original *Star Wars* movie and you walk into a room where a friend is watching it. You come in towards the end, and the very first thing you see is Luke Skywalker firing his proton torpedo and destroying the Death Star. "What kind of story is this!" you protest. "This is *horrific*! That guy with the bad haircut and the wooden delivery is a monster! He just killed thousands of people!" What you're missing is the *bigger picture*: the evil of the Empire and the destruction the Death Star has wrought as it has destroyed planets and innocent people. Locate the act of judgement within the bigger story, and it looks very different.

Retell the Gospel

As I read the Bible, I'm struck by the parallels between the Old Testament and New Testament. Remember that your friend may not know that the Bible was written over a sweeping timeline of

---

7 Genesis 15:12-16.

1,500 years. And one fascinating parallel is that in Hebrew, the names *Jesus* and *Joshua* are the same, with the same meaning: "the Lord saves." So in both halves of the Bible, a guy with the same name goes to war against evil. Joshua's war against evil was one that used the sword—and was a temporary victory. At best, it pointed forward to the need for a much greater battle to come. And in that much greater battle, Jesus warred against evil not with the sword but with self-sacrificial love. Jesus destroys evil once and for all by laying down power and allowing violence to do its worst to him. Even as he hung on the cross, he publicly forgave his enemies who had nailed him there.

And talk of enemies is sobering, isn't it? Because as we ask questions about the Bible and especially the Old Testament, it's easy to sit in judgement on it, assuming we are basically the good guys. But I'll say to my friend, "I wonder whether it's struck you that the Bible doesn't let us off the hook but tells us that we are *all* God's enemies because we've turned our backs on him. Thankfully the God of the Bible is, in Jesus, a God who loved his enemies and laid down his life for them. If we put our trust in him, he offers to make us—his enemies—his friends."

Equip Your Friend

As with the suffering question, the thoughts I shared above have barely scratched the surface. There is so much more to say and there are many more questions your friend may have. So here are some resources I've found helpful to pass to friends who have raised this question. First, a couple of books: Joshua Ryan Butler's *The Skeletons in God's Closet: The Mercy of Hell, the Surprise of Judgment, the Hope of Holy War* and David Lamb's *God Behaving*

Badly: Is the God of the Old Testament Angry, Sexist and Racist? For those who prefer watching to reading, the Solas *Short Answers* series has some helpful episodes on this topic—search for "Old Testament" at www.solas-cpc.org.

Example #3: The Uniqueness of Jesus in a World of Other Faiths

Our third example is a question I hear ever more frequently given the pluralistic world we live in: "How can you claim that Christianity is uniquely true, given there are so many other religions?" (Or more bluntly, "Aren't Christians arrogant for their insistence that it's their way or the highway?")

Sympathise

Again, it's important to build a connection with the person asking the question—not least because they may have friends or family members in other faiths. I remember once being asked this question by a Christian student who was struggling with this issue because her best friend was a Muslim. Asking your friend *why* they ask this question may be especially helpful as it can bring out any personal connection. And I'll often talk about friends and colleagues who are in different faith traditions, my love and respect for them, and so forth.

Hidden Assumptions

There are, of course, lots of assumptions in this question. First up is the issue of assuming that only Christians make exclusive claims. So I'll often ask, "What precisely is it about *Christian* exclusivity that you find difficult? After all, Muslims, Buddhists, Jews—even

atheists—think that their beliefs are true and that others are therefore wrong. Even if you try to say *all* religions are true, you're
excluding those who think only one is. Indeed, I wonder if there's
something about the very nature of truth that makes it exclusive?
Paris is either the capital of France or it isn't; the freezing point
of water at sea level is either 0°C or it isn't; the plastic dinosaur is
either in the salad bowl or it isn't—and so on. Perhaps we shouldn't
be surprised that truth is also exclusive when it comes to religion?"

Apply the Bible

One problem here is that there's a lot of confusion about the word
god, and we can sometimes assume that everybody means the same
thing when they talk about believing (or disbelieving) in "god."
But the Bible is really clear that there are lots of competing ideas
about God, so it's crucial to know *which* god we are talking about.

Furthermore, whilst many people will say things like "But maybe
every religion leads to God," I would argue that *only* the Bible
claims we can get to God. Some religions teach they can lead you
to nonexistence, the annihilation of self. Some, like Islam, promise
they can lead you to Paradise—an eternal life which the Qur'an
describes in terms of rivers of wine, fruit trees, crystal clear foun-
tains of water, and beautiful young women for the men—but God
is very much absent from the picture. By contrast, only the Bible
offers the promise of an eternal life of close communion with God.
Unique to the Bible is the teaching that God is deeply relational.
The God of the Bible walks with Adam and Eve in Genesis, dwells
with his people in the age to come in Revelation, and stepped into
history, personally, in the person of Jesus as he came to deal with
our brokenness and rebellion that separates us from him.

Retell the Gospel

Mention of Jesus, of course, reminds us of something crucial—and I will often ask, "Have you ever wondered about the fact that all this talk of exclusivity comes *from Jesus*? It's Jesus who said, 'I am the way, the truth, and the life; nobody comes to God the Father except through me.'[8] Christians are simply doing our best to faithfully follow what he said and share with others the news of what Jesus makes possible."

Finally, I will sometimes add the observation that for all the ways this is often framed as being a *religious* question ("Do all religions lead to God?"), Jesus was, in many ways, arguably the most anti-religious founder of any major religion, spending most of his time not sucking up to the religious elites of his day but critiquing them, loudly and publicly. Why? Because religion can be really dangerous, leading us to assume that if we think or do the right stuff, we can climb our way upwards to heaven (often looking down on others on our way up). Religion also often becomes *all about us*: "Look at *my* good works, you bunch of lightweights!" By contrast, the good news of the Bible is that it's not all about us but all about Jesus. The God of the Bible doesn't ask us to climb up to him, but in Jesus he climbed down to us. Do all religions lead to God? Maybe *no* religion leads to God, but *God* can lead us to God, and he has done so in the person of Jesus.

Equip Your Friend

As with our other two questions, this is a huge topic, and it can be worth having a few books and resources to hand that you can pass on. Three books that I've found helpful are *Three Theories of*

---

8 John 14:6.

Everything written by former Buddhist monk turned Christian Ellis Potter; *Seeking Allah, Finding Jesus,* Nabeel Qureshi's powerful autobiography of his journey from Islam to Christianity; and my own (shameless plug!) *Do Muslims and Christians Worship the Same God?* If a video would be more appropriate for your friend, again check out the Solas *Short Answers* series—search for "religions" at www.solas-cpc.org.

The Purpose of Answering Questions

With practice, you can use the SHARE approach with almost any question about your faith. Just remember, this isn't a legalistic set of rules to be followed but an easy-to-remember framework to help guide your conversation with a questioner.

As we seek to answer the questions of our friends and colleagues, it's also crucial to remember the goal. We are not trying to win an argument, nor strut like a peacock showing our intellectual feathers ("Tremble before my answers, ye pagans, and believe!"). And we are certainly not labouring under the ludicrous assumption that we can somehow argue people into God's Kingdom. So what are we doing? As Austin Farrer—pastor, theologian, and friend of C. S. Lewis—helpfully put it,

> Though argument does not create conviction, the lack of it destroys belief. What seems to be proved may not be embraced; but what no one shows the ability to defend is quickly abandoned. Rational argument does not create belief, but it maintains a climate in which belief may flourish.[9]

---

9 Austin Farrer, "The Christian Apologist," in Jocelyn Gibb, ed., *Light on C. S. Lewis* (New York: Harcourt, Brace & World, 1965), 26.

Or think of it another way. Imagine that I suddenly come into a large inheritance—perhaps a distant cousin got surprised by a maddened crocodile in a flowerbed and left me a small fortune in his will. In sheer excitement, I blow most of the cash on buying a cottage up in lake country, sight unseen.

When I finally get to visit my new purchase, I rush out to the back, looking forward to the amazing view of the lake the realtor promised. But there's no view to be seen: no lake, no mountains— *nothing*. Just at that point my best friend calls to ask me how the cottage is, and I start ranting at the duplicity of my real estate agent and muttering dark threats about hiding crocodiles in his shrubbery. "There's no view to be seen," I yell into the phone, "just loads of overgrown bushes!"

"Wait right there," my friend says. "I'll drive out and see you. I think I know the problem."

An hour later, my friend turns up in his truck and produces a chain saw.[10] Marching round to the back of my cottage, he looks at the bushes, says, "I suspected as much, darned know-nothing Brit," fires up the chain saw, and proceeds to clear away a decade of growth. And as he does so, lo and behold, the lake view materialises. It was there all along. All that was needed was some extreme pruning.[11]

This is what we're doing when we're answering people's questions about faith, when we're engaging in what is often called *apologetics*, giving an answer and a reason for the hope we have. We can't create faith by what we do, but we can do a little bush clearing. We can, with wisdom, humility, kindness, and the Holy Spirit's empowering, maybe remove some of the debris that prevents people from seeing Jesus clearly.

---

[10] A clever trick, and so much more impressive than rabbits.

[11] Which sounds like a great idea for a TV show: *Extreme Pruning with Bear Grylls*.

For those of us who are perhaps inclined to lean a bit too hard on arguments and risk drifting into the assumption that we're not bush clearing but actually creating the view, or at least dragging people into the lake, C. S. Lewis's "The Apologist's Evening Prayer" is a humbling reminder to keep our feet on the ground:

From all my lame defeats and oh! much more
From all the victories that I seemed to score;
From cleverness shot forth on Thy behalf
At which, while angels weep, the audience laugh;
From all my proofs of Thy divinity,
Thou, who wouldst give no sign, deliver me.

Thoughts are but coins. Let me not trust, instead
Of Thee, their thin-worn image of Thy head.
From all my thoughts, even from my thoughts of Thee,
O thou fair Silence, fall, and set me free.
Lord of the narrow gate and the needle's eye,
Take from me all my trumpery lest I die.[12]

But once we have listened to our friend's question, asked good questions of our own, used the steps in SHARE to help them explore an answer, and engaged in a little bush clearing, what next? In the next chapter, we'll discover some helpful ways to introduce Jesus into the conversation.

---

[12] THE APOLOGISTS EVENING PRAYER by C. S. Lewis copyright © C. S. Lewis Pte. Ltd. Reprinted by permission.

CHAPTER 13

BRINGING IT BACK TO JESUS

A few Christmases ago, my wife had the bright idea of buying our kids a LEGO nativity set. They loved it, for who wouldn't want all the excitement of the Christmas story rendered in garishly coloured plastic bricks?[1] She then had the further idea of dividing the set into twenty-five groups of pieces and using it as an Advent calendar. Now, each year as we approach Christmas, the nativity gets constructed on our kitchen shelf, day by day, plastic piece by plastic piece. (Although occasionally we have to remove dinosaurs, robots, or Imperial stormtroopers which have somehow found their way into the LEGO brick stable.)

One Christmas morning, I came into the kitchen to discover my daughter, then aged about four, playing with the nativity set

---

[1] Somebody has taken this idea from the foothills of possibility way up into the mountains of madness and modelled most of the Bible's stories in LEGO. See www.thebrickbibleforkids.com.

on the table. But I happened to notice that the angel Gabriel had vanished from his customary place on the stable roof and was lying prostrate on the kitchen floor.

"What happened to Gabriel?" I asked as I retrieved the little plastic figure and reattached his wings.

"Daddy," said Caitriona, wearing her Very Serious Face, "he's down there because he was a bad angel."

"A bad angel?"

"Yes. The Lord told him to do something, and he didn't do it."

"Really?"

"Yes! So I smited him."

"Smote, love, smote," I automatically corrected whilst wondering if our daughter had been reading too much of some parts of the Old Testament at bedtime. It was then that I noticed another absentee. The baby Jesus was missing from his little LEGO crib, and it took fifteen minutes of searching before we found him hanging out in the LEGO Friends kitten grooming set.

Sometimes it can be hard to keep Jesus in the right place, front and centre where he belongs, especially when he is surrounded by lots of other things that can distract us from keeping the main thing the main thing. And this isn't just a danger at Christmas. It can also be a risk when it comes to evangelism. We must be careful that—in our desire to listen well, ask great questions, have good conversations, answer our friends' objections, and present Christianity as reasonable—we don't forget the primary task is to introduce people to Jesus. Everything else is simply a means to an end.

More than Mere Religion

Ensuring that we keep the focus on Jesus as we talk about our faith is crucial because if we don't, the danger is that the conversation will subtly shift (at least in our friends' minds) and become all about "religion." And for many of our secular friends, religion is a huge turnoff and one that causes an instant recoil, like being offered a slug-paste sandwich at a party.

Among the most common reactions I hear when I engage people in conversation is either "I'm not religious" or the even stronger "I *hate* religion." It's not simply that huge numbers of people don't consider themselves religious anymore; it's that religion is seen as a negative thing. For sure, we can debate the difference between "good religion" and "bad religion," but that may not be *flogging* a dead horse so much as trying to win the Kentucky Derby with a pony that has long since decomposed into a pile of bones and a few pots of glue.

Thankfully, as the first Christians took the story of Jesus' life, death, and resurrection across the ancient world, they didn't use the word *religion* for that message. Instead they chose a far more helpful term, the Greek word *euangelion*, which in English is usually translated "gospel." And that word doesn't mean "religion" but rather "good news." As theologian and historian Tom Wright puts it,

> Many people today assume that Christianity is . . . a religion, a moral system, a philosophy. In other words, they assume that Christianity is about advice. But it wasn't and it isn't. Christianity is, simply, good news. It is the news that something has happened as a result of which the world is a different place. . . . One can debate the merits of a religion, moral system, or philosophy, but a news event is discussed in a different way. Either the event happened or it didn't; if it did happen, either it means what people say it means or it doesn't.[2]

---

[2] N. T. Wright, *Simply Good News: Why the Gospel Is News and What Makes It Good* (London: SPCK, 2015), 16–17.

There are also some profound differences between religion—at least in the way that most people commonly understand the term, or in the way that other religious systems use it—and the gospel. Author and pastor Tim Keller helpfully lays out some of the key differences:[3]

- Religion says, "I obey—therefore I'm accepted." The gospel says, "I'm accepted, and therefore I obey."
- Religion says, "My motivation is fear and insecurity." The gospel says, "My motivation is grateful joy."
- Religion says, "When things go wrong, I get angry at God or myself, because being good should result in a comfortable life." The gospel says, "When things go wrong, I struggle, but I know that all my punishment fell on Jesus, and I also know that God loves me and is with me through trials."
- Religion says, "My identity is based on performance and image." The gospel says, "My identity is not based on performance but on God's love for me in Christ."
- Religion says, "My prayer life largely consists of petition, because the purpose of prayer is control." The gospel says, "My prayer life consists of lots of praise and adoration, because the purpose of prayer is fellowship with Christ."
- Religion says, "My self-view swings between confidence (when I live up to my standards) and failure (when I don't)." The gospel says, "My self-view is not based on my achievements but on Christ, in whom I am simultaneously a sinner but saved—I am so bad that Jesus *had* to die for me; I am so loved that he was *glad* to die for me."

---

3 Adapted from Timothy Keller, *Center Church: Doing Balanced, Gospel-Centered Ministry in Your City* (Grand Rapids: Zondervan, 2012), 65.

Do you see now why it's important to be clear in our minds about exactly what it is we are aiming to share with our friends when we talk with them? We are not sharing an idea, or some advice, or a fifteen-step self-help programme. In fact, we're not aiming to share with them a *what* at all, but rather a *whom*. Because, in a nutshell, what is the gospel—the Good News? Jesus.

This is not to fall into the oversimplified soundbite trap that we talked about in chapter 6 (simply parroting "Jesus is the answer" unthinkingly to every question, including "Do you know how to get blueberry stains off a hamster?"). Rather, the gospel says that Jesus is *everything*. He's the question and the answer—and everything in between. The gospel *is* Jesus.

Learning from Paul

So if Jesus is the gospel, if our joyful task is to introduce people to Jesus (not forgetting that he already knows our friends, as he created and died for them!), how do we do it? In one of my favourite passages in the book of Acts (which we've already looked at briefly), the apostle Paul demonstrates a brilliant model of how to do this in a culture and with people who have no history of Christianity.

In Acts 17, we find Paul on a missionary trip with Silas and Timothy. But Paul gets separated from his friends, and whilst waiting for them to catch up, he ends up with some time to kill in Athens. Rather than getting badly lost in the suburbs, chased by a mad dog, and then outrageously shortchanged by a taxi driver (which was my experience last time I got stuck in Athens), Paul puts his time to much better use:

> While Paul was waiting for them in Athens, he was
> greatly distressed to see that the city was full of idols. So

he reasoned in the synagogue with both Jews and God-fearing Greeks, as well as in the market-place day by day with those who happened to be there. A group of Epicurean and Stoic philosophers began to debate with him. Some of them asked, "What is this babbler trying to say?" Others remarked, "He seems to be advocating foreign gods." They said this because Paul was preaching the good news about Jesus and the resurrection. Then they took him and brought him to a meeting of the Areopagus, where they said to him, "May we know what this new teaching is that you are presenting? You are bringing some strange ideas to our ears, and we would like to know what they mean." (All the Athenians and the foreigners who lived there spent their time doing nothing but talking about and listening to the latest ideas.)

Paul then stood up in the meeting of the Areopagus and said: "People of Athens! I see that in every way you are very religious. For as I walked around and looked carefully at your objects of worship, I even found an altar with this inscription: TO AN UNKNOWN GOD. So you are ignorant of the very thing you worship—and this is what I am going to proclaim to you.

"The God who made the world and everything in it is the Lord of heaven and earth and does not live in temples built by human hands. And he is not served by human hands, as if he needed anything. Rather, he himself gives everyone life and breath and everything else. From one man he made all the nations, that they should inhabit the whole earth; and he marked out their appointed times in history and the boundaries of their lands. God did this so that they would seek him and perhaps reach out for him and find him, though he is not far from any one of us. 'For in him we live and move and have our being.' As some of your own poets have said, 'We are his offspring.'

"Therefore since we are God's offspring, we should not think that the divine being is like gold or silver or stone—an image made by human design and skill. In the past God overlooked such ignorance, but now he commands all people everywhere to repent. For he has set a day when he will judge the world with justice by the man he has appointed. He has given proof of this to everyone by raising him from the dead."

When they heard about the resurrection of the dead, some of them sneered, but others said, "We want to hear you again on this subject." At that, Paul left the Council. Some of the people became followers of Paul and believed. Among them was Dionysius, a member of the Areopagus, also a woman named Damaris, and a number of others.

ACTS 17:16-34

When it comes to thinking about how to bring Jesus into a conversation, I believe there are four key lessons we can learn from Paul here.

First, notice that Paul took the time to observe and to understand. He walked around the city. He looked at the temples, statues, and idols. Rather than assume he knew what the Athenians believed, he invested some time in finding out firsthand. In the same way, when it comes to sharing Jesus with our friends, it can be incredibly helpful to do the same—to find out what they believe, what gets them out of bed in the morning, what makes them tick. How can we do that? Well, back in chapter 5 we briefly met these four questions:

- Do you think there's some kind of god, and if so, what is god like?
- What does it mean to be a human being?
- What's gone wrong with the world?
- What's the solution?

I encourage you to try these out with a friend. One easy way to do this is to say that you're reading a book about how we can talk about our beliefs more helpfully with others, and the book has encouraged you to interview somebody with different religious beliefs to yours. As you ask your friend these questions, take a real interest in their answers. Ask follow-up questions. If you're not sure what they mean, clarify. A good goal is to be able to summarise your friend's beliefs in such a way that they'd recognise the summary and say, "Yes! That's right!" As you do this, I hope you will find, as Paul did, that the more you discover, the more this moves you to compassion and a deeper desire to share Jesus with them.

Second, Paul found a point of contact in the Greek culture—one from which he could build a bridge. You see, the Athenians were so religious that they were worried that in all their frenetic temple building, they'd missed a minor deity. They were concerned they might offend Kevin the God of Cutlery, or Hilary the Goddess of Lost Causes or something, so they had tried to cover their bases by building an Altar to an Unknown God. This enabled Paul to say, "Well done on your desire to worship—that's brilliant! But that altar shows you have no idea who you're trying to worship. So let me tell you about the *real* God."

Third, Paul was not afraid to critique the beliefs of the culture. He was not *so* concerned with bridge building that he avoided any confrontation or challenge. Likewise, as we talk with our friends, we shouldn't be afraid to gently but firmly say why we think their beliefs don't quite hang together. After all, having built a bridge, we want to encourage people to cross it.

Fourth, Paul connects the other side of the bridge he has built to Jesus. In particular, he attempts to show the Athenians that what they were looking for—a connection with the divine—is something that is only possible in and through Jesus and his redemptive work on the cross, a fact proven by the resurrection. What Paul models for us here is something we can do too: looking for the desires, hopes, and aspirations of our friends and showing how ultimately they can only be met in Jesus.

In his book *Plugged In: Connecting Your Faith with What You Watch, Read, and Play*, my friend Dan Strange similarly draws from Paul's sermon in Athens and then applies it to lots of contemporary topics. For example, consider sport—which dominates the lives of so many of our friends. If you're talking with a colleague who is a huge sports fan, you might begin by *understanding*—finding out why they care so much about playing or watching. You might then *bridge build* and observe how sport gives many people a sense of identity, belonging, and hope. But then you might also offer a bit of a *critique*: This is all very well, but what happens when our team loses? If our self-esteem is based purely on performance, doesn't this often result in pride or crippling despair? And doesn't sport lead at times to a horrible tribalism, sometimes even spilling over into violence? Finally, you can *evangelise*, observing that the good news of Jesus is that our self-esteem and identity are not based on success (there are no winners or losers in the church). If you are a Jesus follower, you can still be a sports fan, but confident that if your team crash and burn, your identity remains secure, and if they totally ace it, you can celebrate without denigrating others.[4]

Jesus and the Longing at the Heart of Religion

The same approach works if you're talking with somebody from a different religion, where if you listen carefully enough, you'll find a hope, desire, or longing that the religion in question simply fails to answer. A few years ago, a friend of mine fell into conversation with a Buddhist monk he was sitting next to on a flight. My friend asked his fellow passenger lots of questions about his faith, and the Buddhist kept returning to the idea that a central tenet of his belief was that all desire had to be eliminated, because desire is the cause of suffering. Earlier the monk had mentioned his family, so my friend asked, "You have children then?"

"Yes, three," the monk replied.

"And you love them and want them to be happy, I imagine?"

"Dearly!"

"So would it be fair to say that your goal would be to eliminate that desire too?" There was an awkward silence, and my friend followed by asking, "It also occurs to me that one of the world's most famous Buddhists, the Dalai Lama, has talked about his desire for the freedom of the Tibetan people. Isn't that a worthy desire?"

"We're not really encouraged in Buddhism to ask these kinds of questions," the monk said sadly.

---

4 Daniel Strange, *Plugged In: Connecting Your Faith with What You Watch, Read, and Play* (Epsom, UK: Good Book Company, 2019), 117–140.

My friend was able to then suggest that rather than eliminating desire entirely, what we want is somebody who can help us deal with the unhelpful, bad, or wrong desires—which was why he is a follower of Jesus. And in Jesus, too, arguably we see an answer to the problem of suffering far more profound than trying fruitlessly to tackle it on our own. "And that reminds me," my friend said, "of what Jesus once said: 'I have come that they may have life, and have it to the full.'"

That little remark my friend made—"That reminds me . . ."—can be another helpful tool in our evangelistic toolbox, as it offers a natural way of bridging a conversation to Jesus and bringing him front and centre.

"That Reminds Me of Something Jesus Said . . ."

One way to do this is to look for an opportunity to say, "That reminds me of something Jesus said." My friend Jenny once told me the story of how, as she got into a cab after a church service, the cab driver asked, "Have you just been in there?" jerking his thumb at the church.

"Yes," Jenny replied.

"What's a young person like you want with all that religious stuff?" the cabbie muttered. "Religion is just a psychological crutch for those who are weak, feeble, and need a bit of comfort in life."

"Well, thanks for that," Jenny said, "but your comment reminds me of something Jesus said. On one occasion he said that anybody who wanted to follow him should deny themselves, take up their cross, and be willing to give up their life. You know, I find following Jesus really hard work—it'd be far easier in many ways if I just went with the flow. But then, maybe only dead things go with the flow. What do you think?"

One of the most surprising examples of a "that reminds me of something Jesus said" comment comes from, of all people, an atheist. In his book *The Madness of Crowds: Gender, Race and Identity*, the British journalist Douglas Murray has a fascinating chapter lamenting that our culture is incredibly judgemental and has forgotten how to forgive. Murray writes, "[Social media] appears able to cause catastrophes but not to heal them, to wound but not to remedy. . . . The question that the internet age has still not begun to contend with [is] how, if ever, is our age able to forgive?"[5]

As he explores this question, Douglas talks about how he is *reminded* of Christianity and particularly of Jesus' dialogue with Peter in Matthew 18 concerning how many times one is supposed to forgive. What, Douglas wonders out loud, does a world that seems to have entirely forgotten this virtue or possibility look like? I've used this same connection—between our need for forgiveness and what Jesus has to offer—many times in conversations myself, often using a "that reminds me of something Jesus said" link to do it.

"That Reminds Me of Something Jesus Did . . ."

A second way you can easily bridge a conversation to Jesus is by looking for an opportunity to make a connection to something Jesus did. Just a couple of days before I typed these words, a friend and I were talking to a university student whose biggest obstacle to considering Christianity was the many examples of church leaders abusing their power for personal gain—whether financial or sexual. Sadly, you don't have to do a lot of googling to find numerous

---

5 Douglas Murray, *The Madness of Crowds: Gender, Race and Identity* (London: Bloomsbury, 2019), 174, 176. If you have the time, watch the fascinating discussion between Murray and Christian theologian N. T. Wright: www.thebigconversation.show/mythmiraclesandidentity.

news stories of church leaders who were not so much wolves in sheep's clothing as wolves in wolves' clothing. How, this student asked, could anybody possibly take Christianity seriously when some of its leaders behaved like this?

There were many things I *could* have said in reply, but I felt the only answer with any weight at this point was to put the focus not on the stupidity of humanity but on the beauty of Christ. And so I said, "I share your utter disgust at these stories, not least because they're so totally antithetical to how Jesus behaved. You know, I'm reminded of the story of Jesus washing his disciples' feet, something that was unheard of for a Jewish leader to do." We then talked a little about what servant leadership looks like, and I was in time able to add, "All this also reminds me of what Jesus did on the cross. Here was somebody with ultimate power, yet he laid it all down, did not victimize others but became a victim himself. Any leader whose leadership does not make you think of that doesn't deserve the label 'Christian.'" As we ended the conversation, we were able to give the student a copy of Mark's Gospel, in which, I said, we find some of Jesus' most powerful words on this: "For even the Son of Man did not come to be served, but to serve, and to give his life as a ransom for many."[6]

Similarly, "that reminds me of something Jesus did" can be helpful when talking with those who have no time for religion. I have a friend in Toronto who, whenever he meets somebody who makes a negative remark about the corrosive effect of organised religion, will say something like "So let me get this straight, you don't like religion?"

"No, I hate it!"

---

6 Mark 10:45.

"The odd thing is, this reminds me of something Jesus did. In Mark's Gospel, the earliest of the four first-century biographies we have of Jesus, there's this amazing account of how Jesus got so angry at the way the Temple—which was supposed to be the place people connected with God—had been turned by the religious leaders into a 'den of robbers.' And so Jesus literally took a whip and cleared out the Temple courtyard, with the result that the religious authorities decided they needed to kill him. It seems from this that maybe Jesus had a problem with organised religion too. Maybe you should take a closer look at Jesus?"

Over the years, my friend has found that this approach can open up numerous conversations, as people are surprised to discover that Jesus had little time for dead, desiccated religion and the way it really just served the powerful religious elites. And if you can get people curious enough to read the Gospels for themselves, God can do amazing things.

"That Reminds Me of a Story Jesus Told . . ."

Finally, we can bring Jesus into the heart of a discussion by saying, "That reminds me of a story Jesus told." I have found this especially effective with Muslim friends, who are often deeply intrigued by Jesus (there are approximately ninety verses in the Qur'an about Jesus, although the Jesus found there is very different from the Jesus of the Gospels). I have had many conversations with Muslim friends where the issue of Jesus comes up, and they will ask why Christians believe, as we do, that Jesus wasn't just a prophet but was actually divine. Now you can try to answer that kind of question with clever theological answers, but sometimes I've found it more fruitful to say, "I'm encouraged we're talking about who Jesus was—because that was the question Jesus himself liked to ask people. Who do *you* think Jesus was?"

"I'm a Muslim. I believe that Jesus, peace be upon him, was a prophet of Allah."

"But was that what Jesus himself would have said? I'm reminded of a story Jesus told . . ." And then I will often read Jesus' parable of the tenants in the vineyard from Mark 12—a story that has massive identity questions at the heart of it. Who does Jesus think he is in the story? If the messengers are the prophets, who does that make the son in the story? And if Jesus considered *himself* the son, what does the fact that the tenants kill the son mean? By reading the story and asking those kinds of questions, before you know it, you're having a Bible study right there with your Muslim friend. And you're not arguing about what *you* think; you're discussing what Jesus taught, said, and did.

Another time I recall a "that reminds me of a story Jesus told" comment being helpful occurred a few years ago when I was at a men's breakfast event a local church was running. Lots of folks had invited guests, and I was due to give a short talk on "The Problem of Happiness: Why We Look for Joy in All the Wrong Places." Whilst we were waiting for the bacon and eggs to arrive, I got chatting to the person next to me and asked why he'd come to the event. "My neighbour invited me," he replied, "and I thought I'd give it a go—I haven't set foot inside a church since I was a kid, but the topic really intrigued me."

"What do you mean by that?" I asked (as I'd read chapter 8 and taken notes).

"Well, it's like this. For the past ten years, I've been pursuing a bit of a dream. My goal was to pay off the mortgage early so we'd be debt-free as a family. So I worked three jobs, worked every hour there was, really. Saved every spare penny. And last week—last week, I made it! I went into the bank, wrote a cheque, and paid off the house. Five years early too!"

"Well done!" I said. "That's impressive! You must be *really* happy!"

"No," my new friend replied, "not really. Odd, isn't it? I thought paying off the house would be the happiest day of my life. But the moment I wrote the cheque, I suddenly realised with horror I had nothing to live for. It's a bit like that moment in *The Princess Bride*, where the Spanish swordsman, Inigo Montoya, finally fulfils his life's dream and kills the man who murdered his father. He says, 'I have been in the revenge business so long, now that it's over, I don't know what to do with the rest of my life.' I've been looking for happiness in the wrong place but am not sure where the right place is. That's why I've come to this event."

Again, there were many things I could have said (such as "Inconceivable!"), but in the end I ran with "You know, this reminds me of a story Jesus told." I then retold Jesus' parable of the wise and foolish builders, which enabled me to say that Jesus knows full well our tendency to build our lives on things that let us down. Then I shared the difference it had made to my life when I'd discovered the importance of making Jesus the foundation on which to build, other than those things that will only ultimately disappoint.

The Compass in the Conversation

I'm a keen hiker, and some years ago I was wandering around the extensive rocky upland behind Scafell Pike, England's tallest mountain, when the fog began to blow in. Soon everything was grey, and I couldn't see more than ten feet in front of me. Unfazed, I pulled out my compass and began to follow the right bearing, only the farther I walked, the more it began to feel *wrong*. Although the compass *said* that I was walking the right way, all my instincts told me otherwise. So I did what any man does when lost and faced with the choice of following the technology or following a hunch—I followed the hunch and soon was badly lost. Sure that the path lay farther to the left, I kept correcting my direction, convinced the compass had gone mad. Suddenly I came upon a rock I recognised from where I'd stopped earlier for a cup of tea, and at that point the wind picked up and the fog lifted, revealing that for the past twenty minutes I had been walking in one large loop.

When we take our eyes off the compass, we have a tendency to walk in circles, and the same is true of conversations about faith, which can also wander in fruitless loops. But if we bring Jesus into the conversation and use him as our fixed point, then sometimes those conversations can really go places. Ultimately, none of this is about us, our arguments, or our clever questions, but it's about people wanting to read the Gospels for themselves, being willing to give Jesus a fair look, and asking themselves as they read, "Who does Jesus think he is? Do I believe him?" After all, the choices are fairly stark: Was he a liar? Was he totally nuts? Or was he really God with us?

But as you bring the conversation back to Jesus, as you're "reminded" of things that Jesus said and did, and as you point your friends into the Gospels, what happens if they struggle with the disparity between Jesus and the Christians they know? How can we help people to look past the mess that the church has sometimes made of things and see Jesus? It's to that question that we'll turn in chapter 14.

HOW NOT TO BE A CRUNCHY CHRISTIAN

A FEW YEARS AGO, my family and I were holidaying in the English Lake District, and over our week there we befriended another family, whom we met when we took our kids to play in a local park.[1] We spent lots of time with this other family, our kids played with their kids, we hiked and had a few meals together. Over various conversations, questions came up about our faith, but on the final evening, I was asked a question I had never before encountered. Midway through a rather dubious curry, the wife looked at us, puzzled, and said, "I simply can't work you two out. You're clearly very into this Jesus thing, but you're not . . . *crunchy*. What's different about you?"

I paused, a forkful of chicken vindaloo halfway to my mouth. "Crunchy? What do you mean?"

---

[1] We've found that having small children is an easy way to meet other families because "I'm sorry my child whacked your child with a stick whilst playing Pirates and Real Estate Agents—please don't sue!" is a terrific opening line when waiting for the ambulance to arrive.

"Oh, you know, crunchy Christians!"

"I have no idea what you're talking about. What are crunchy Christians? Some kind of cannibalistic breakfast snack?" (My wife kicked me under the table. Apparently this was not the time for dad jokes.[2])

"Oh, you know what I mean. The kind of religious people you just can't have normal conversations with. They're always so deathly serious, or judging you, or tutting at things you say, or behaving like total hypocrites, or trying to press horribly designed leaflets about something at their church into your hands. In the end you give up and avoid them. They're *crunchy*."

As I paused to consider this, the curry slowly dissolving the metal of my fork, it occurred to me that this is, sadly, not an unusual sentiment. Tragically, Christians and the church do sometimes have a bit of an image problem, whether it's due to the dramatic stories of clergy financial and sexual abuses that have made headline news, the take-no-prisoners way some Christians have badly entangled faith and politics, or simply really awkward and cheesy evangelism. And let's admit, there have been some terrible forms of evangelism over the years—including plastering fish symbols on the fenders of our cars and then cutting off people in traffic or photobombing tourists whilst waving a "John 3:16" sign.[3] It may be worth remembering that if you're being persecuted or criticised for your faith, it doesn't *automatically* mean you're being faithful; it could be because you're being an idiot. Remember that the Bible tells us to be fools for Christ[4] but not jerks for Jesus.

---

[2] Sadly, I am regularly informed by my family that *no* time is the time for dad jokes.

[3] This really is a thing: see Martin Saunders, "Seven Terrible Evangelism Ideas . . . and a Few That Might Work Better," *Christian Today*, March 26, 2015.

[4] 1 Corinthians 4:10.

The reality is that people *will* judge the message by its messengers. We can ask great questions, we can listen well, we can learn to have good conversations—and all of those are important and will help decrunchify us. Nevertheless, if people see a disconnect between our words and our lives, if what they see on the *outside* doesn't correlate with what they hear from the *inside*, then they're going to be deeply suspicious—and rightly so.

That's the *bad* news.

But thankfully, there is some *good* news. For as the French theologian Étienne Gilson memorably put it, "It does not depend on us that [the gospel] be believed, but we can do very much toward making it respected."[5] For whilst it is possible to do considerable damage to the credibility of the gospel by being a crunchy Christian, the opposite is also true: living out our faith in Christ honestly, openly, and with integrity can create a real openness for the gospel.

In his book *The Righteous Mind: Why Good People Are Divided by Politics and Religion*, psychologist Jonathan Haidt offers the metaphor of a rider and an elephant to help explain how we make many of our judgements. We like to *think* we make them by using careful reason, but much of the time they are really instinctive. The Rider of Reason is sitting on top of the Elephant of Intuition—and whilst the rider can attempt to steer the elephant, much of the time the elephant will charge wherever it sees fit. This is why it can sometimes be hard talking to people who hold a very different religious or moral view to our own: we may *think* that our arguments for Christianity are the bee's knees or the spider's elbows, but our sceptical friend refuses to even consider them. The problem, Haidt

---

[5] Étienne Gilson, *A Gilson Reader: Selected Writings* (Garden City, NY: Hanover House, 1957), 48.

would say, is that we're appealing to the *rider*. Listen to Haidt's advice—he's talking in this example about moral discussions, but the same applies to conversations about faith:

> When does the elephant listen to reason? The main way that we change our minds on moral issues is by interacting with other people. We are terrible at seeking evidence that challenges our own beliefs, but other people do us this favor, just as we are quite good at finding errors in other people's beliefs. When discussions are hostile, the odds of change are slight. The elephant leans away from the opponent, and the rider works frantically to rebut the opponent's charges.
>
> But if there is affection, admiration, or a desire to please the other person, then the elephant leans *toward* that person and the rider tries to find the truth in the other person's arguments. The elephant may not often change its direction in response to objections from its *own* rider, but it is easily steered by the mere presence of friendly elephants.[6]

The takeaway here is not that you should swap the fish sticker on the back of your Honda for a sign that says, "I'm a Friendly Elephant for Jesus." Rather, it's a reminder, from a secular psychologist, of 1 Peter 3:15: if we engage people with gentleness and respect, then they are far more likely to be drawn toward us rather than to veer away from us.

One of my favourite examples of this was in a follow-up

---

[6] Jonathan Haidt, *The Righteous Mind: Why Good People Are Divided by Politics and Religion*, (New York: Vintage Books, 2012), 79.

discussion group run by some university students after a mission week in Montreal. It was a mixed group of seekers and sceptics, among whom was Mark, an atheist who had been the first to raise his hand and ask an awkward question after every talk the week before. But as the discussion group met each week, and particularly as a couple of the other atheists in it did their very best to make a nuisance of themselves (whilst the Christians responded with patience and generosity), people began to notice that Mark the Loudmouthed Atheist slowly but surely started speaking up to *defend* Christians and Christianity from some of the attacks others were making. When the follow-up group came to an end, Mark began studying the Bible with a couple of Christians and three months later was baptised. Part of his journey to faith had been that friendly Christian elephants had deeply attracted him! Mark's story reminds me of the words of the nineteenth-century British evangelist Gipsy Smith, who once remarked, "There are five gospels: Matthew, Mark, Luke, John . . . and the life of the individual Christian. Most people will not read the first four."

Five Steps to Becoming Less Crunchy

If at this point you're thinking that this all sounds a bit daunting, do not fear. Be encouraged that all of us have work to do in this area, and there are some simple steps you can try as you seek to become a friendlier elephant.

The first step is to *pray*. Prayer is always the place to begin, as it puts the focus on Christ and reminds us that without his transforming power in our lives, melting the glacial corners of our hearts or knocking the hard edges off the occasional bit of obstinate brickwork, Christianity becomes just a moral self-improvement plan. Gritting your teeth and muttering under your breath, "Must try harder" is more likely to transform your blood pressure than your character. But the Holy Spirit *can* transform even the most curmudgeonly of us. So pray that you'd become more Christlike.

We can also pray that Jesus would help us to love people like he did. Let's be honest, this is a tough one. As somebody once remarked, "Jesus said love your enemies—but they're the last of my worries, it's my colleagues and neighbours that are the toughest!" But it's as sobering as a cup of Klatchian Coffee to reflect on some of the people that Jesus regularly hung around: Matthew and Zacchaeus, who were tax collectors and hated by everybody. James and John, who were always at each other's throats—and probably everybody else's. Simon the Zealot—the clue's in the name: the Zealots were basically terrorists. And that's before we get to the social outcasts, the weirdos, and the guys who smelt of fish. Indeed, the only people who seemed on the whole *not* to be attracted to Jesus were the religious types: the Pharisees and teachers of the law.

Jesus models for us what it means to live a life that is attractive, generous, engaging, and open such that even those whose lifestyles would suggest they'd want nothing to do with him are nevertheless drawn to him. We can pray that the Holy Spirit would soften us and develop the same kind of character in us. So start with prayer.

Second, practice developing the virtues of transparency and honesty—be open about your doubts and your failings. If your colleagues and friends pick up the idea that you've aspirations to be an otherworldly saint who floats around an inch above the ground whilst casting aspersions on lesser mortals, they'll avoid you like a helping of roadkill stew. But if you're open about the fact you're *not* superhuman, maybe they'll be more likely to realise that Christianity is not about perfection but about grace.

This is especially important when you mess up. A friend of mine told me of an occasion when he'd made a mistake at work and in panic had lied in a meeting to cover what he'd done. Afterwards a colleague called him out on it, and rather than try to defend himself, my friend had said, "I'm really sorry. Not just because I let the team down but also because I'm a Christian, and I try to live a life that models Jesus' values. And lying is not one of them. I'm sorry I've given you a poor impression of what a Christian looks like." That admission defused the whole situation, and my friend then followed up by saying, "Look, would you in future do me a favour? If you see me behaving in a way that doesn't look Christian to you, would you please tell me?" By not hiding his failings, even inviting his colleagues to challenge him when he messed up, over time he was able to open many more conversations about faith. Because our identity is based on what Jesus thinks of us, Christians can surely be people who are not afraid of admitting our failures.

Third, do your very best to be an excellent friend, neighbour, and colleague. In workplace settings this is especially vital. People notice if you're known to be a Christian but also have a reputation for being a team member who works hard, does a great job, and doesn't talk down to others, insult customers, take short cuts, cheat the company, or do any of the other everyday grubbiness that can happen in many workplaces. Think of the example of Daniel, who even whilst in captivity in Babylon worked so hard and faithfully that he rose up the ranks and found favour with King Nebuchadnezzar himself.

Fourth, look for opportunities to sacrificially serve colleagues and show them something of the love and kindness of God. Sometimes even small things can make a tremendous difference. A friend of mine, Steve, who works in a busy local government office, told me that over the years he's tried to make a habit of looking out for when colleagues are having a bad time or a stressful day, and then he's made them a coffee or left a gift of chocolate on their desk. Little acts of kindness like this build up and can give a tremendous credibility to conversations about faith.

But sometimes there are bigger opportunities to live out the gospel in the workplace. In his book *Every Good Endeavour: Connecting Your Work to God's Work*, Tim Keller tells how, not long after he came to pastor Redeemer Presbyterian Church in New York, he noticed a young woman who would turn up for each service, sit at the back, then dart out without speaking to anybody. One Sunday morning he managed to intercept her before she left, and she explained that she was exploring Christianity—it was interesting and attractive to her, but she wasn't yet a Christian. So Tim asked her how she had come to find the church, and she related the following story.

She worked for a large corporation in Manhattan, and soon after starting work there, she had made a horrendous mistake: a catastrophic, career-ending, wreck-of-the-Hindenburg type of mistake. But rather than fire her on the spot, her boss had gone in to *his* boss and taken responsibility for what she'd done. That had resulted in a lot of trouble—had cost her supervisor reputation and influence—but had saved her job. The next day, she went into his office to thank him and to ask why he'd done it. He tried to brush it off as nothing worth mentioning, but she insisted on knowing what was different about him. She'd worked for plenty of bosses all too quick to take credit for things she'd accomplished, but never had she seen one willing to take the blame for an underling's mess-ups. Finally, her boss quietly said, "I am a Christian. That means among other things that God accepts me because

Jesus Christ took the blame for things that I have done wrong. He did that on the cross. That is why I have the desire and sometimes the ability to take the blame for others." The woman stared at him, amazed. "Which church do you go to?" she asked. Her boss suggested she try Redeemer Presbyterian, and so she went. As Tim puts it,

> His character had been shaped by his experience of grace in the gospel, and it made his behavior as a manager attractive and strikingly different from that of others. This lack of self-interest and ruthlessness on the part of her supervisor was eventually life-transforming to her.[7]

Maybe you won't have an opportunity of that magnitude. But what if you prayed that God might open your eyes to opportunities to sacrificially serve a colleague, friend, or neighbour in even a small way, one that gives them a little glimpse of the goodness and beauty of the gospel?

Fifth, make an effort to build real friendships with those who are not Christians—and not just so you can use them for evangelistic cannon fodder, but so you can love and care for them as Jesus did for those he met. Too often we are so busy with all our Christian activities—or (intentionally or unintentionally) buying into a kind of Christian tribalism—that we only invest in friendships with Christians.

In Matthew 5, Jesus famously told Christians that we are to be "the salt of the earth." In the ancient world, before we'd discovered refrigerators and before fast-food restaurants had worked out how

---

7 Timothy Keller and Katherine Leary Alsdorf, *Every Good Endeavor: Connecting Your Work to God's Work* (New York: Dutton, 2012), 219.

to make food out of plastic, salt had a vital function as a preservative. But in order to work that way, it had to be in contact with the thing it was supposed to preserve. And the same is true when it comes to the gospel. In our everyday lives we need to be mixing with those we want to influence. If we're so busy at church, for example, that we can't do that, maybe we need to rethink some priorities.

Consider also how you can build friendships that cut across the obvious lines. When I lived in Toronto, I had the privilege of speaking at a Christian-Muslim dialogue event organised by a local church and a local mosque. But what fascinated me was how the event came about. Some years before, the assistant pastor at the church had been in the local shopping mall, had popped into a convenience store, and had got chatting to the guy behind the counter, who was a Muslim. They struck up a friendship and began meeting for coffee to talk more. They soon discovered that the pastor's church and the shopkeeper's mosque were two blocks apart, and as the friendship and trust grew, they hit on the idea of seeing if their respective places of worship would be open to launching an annual dialogue event. By the time I spoke there, it had been running for eight years and had grown from a hundred or so attendees to over a thousand—and several Muslims had come to faith in Christ through it. All because a Christian had taken the time to become good friends with a Muslim.

Whilst it is unlikely that most of us will be called by the Lord to organise massive public dialogues with Muslims, perhaps it is still worth asking: Who is the person at work whose beliefs are *most* different to your own? The individual you're *most* naturally likely to avoid? What might it look like to try to build bridges to them, however challenging it might be at first?

When Other Christians (or the Church) Go Wrong

But there is still an elephant in the room, and it is not a friendly one. What happens when— despite our best efforts to show kindness, grace, and hospitality to our colleagues and neighbours, modelling Christ's love by our actions—they still have a negative view of Christianity because of other Christians? I was deeply grateful that the friends we made on holiday didn't consider us *crunchy*, but they still felt that this was a typical adjective to describe the Christians they had encountered. Or I think of the student who recently said to me, "I increasingly find Jesus attractive, but the church—no thanks!" Whether it's bad personal experiences with Christians, horrible scandals involving Christian leaders, or even the historical legacy of the church—everything from the Crusades, to the slave trade, to the Spanish Inquisition—what do we do when the bad example of Christianity is not something we can actually change?

Well, the first principle is don't make excuses or defend. For sure, in the case of history we can sometimes nuance things (there's an argument the Crusades were largely a response to Muslim aggression, or that more people are killed annually by bicycles than were killed by the Spanish Inquisition in three hundred years, or that Arab Muslims enslaved more people in Africa than European Christians), but really, who wants to look like an apologist for awfulness? People won't remember "Oh, my Christian friend explained this really well!" but rather "That Christian tried to justify genocide, torture, and slavery." Like the offer of a cut-price holiday to North Korea: *don't go there.*

Instead, I find it better to do two things. First, apologise. You don't need to apologise *personally* for what happened—after all, you weren't there. But you can express sorrow, shame, and regret that the stupid behaviour of people who wore the badge "Christian" has given your friend a terrible impression of Christianity, of the church, and of Jesus. I often add that I'm ashamed of all this because it's such an utter travesty of Jesus' message. No figure in history was more scathing, critical, or indeed subversive when it came to the question of violence and religion. "Love your enemies and pray for those who persecute you," said Jesus. "If anyone slaps you on the right cheek, turn to them the other cheek also."[8]

And that should tell us something. It should tell us that when somebody behaves appallingly in the name of Jesus, perhaps they've borrowed his name for their own nefarious purposes. After all, we can gently point out to our friends, anybody can *proclaim* themselves to be a Christian, but how do we know if they really are? Indeed, as we look back through history (ancient and modern), we see that the church has a mixed record—it has been linked to terrible atrocities and failures, but it has also been a tremendous force for good.

In the recent Australian documentary *For the Love of God*,[9] the presenters use a helpful analogy. Consider a famous composition of classical music, such as Bach's Cello Suites. Now, you might listen to a world-class cellist, for example the Chinese-American maestro Yo-Yo Ma, play those pieces of music beautifully. Or you could listen to me—a person who is tone-deaf and hasn't picked up a cello for over thirty years, play them badly. But how would you best judge the quality of the Cello Suites themselves? Presumably you can only judge them when the music is played properly, as the composer actually intended.

---

[8] Matthew 5:39, 44.

[9] *For the Love of God: How the Church Is Better and Worse than You Ever Imagined*, directed by Allan Dowthwaite (Sydney: CPX, 2018), video, 90 min. The main writer and presenter, John Dickson, expanded on the material in his book *Bullies and Saints: An Honest Look at the Good and Evil of Christian History* (Grand Rapids, MI: Zondervan Reflective, 2021).

And we can suggest that it's the same when we look at Jesus and the church. We can't truly assess Christianity unless we ask what it has looked like when people have faithfully tried to live out Jesus' message, even at great personal cost to themselves. Yes, there have been bad performances; but it is to the best performances, the authentic performances, that we should look if we want to see Jesus' message in practice.

The one danger to be aware of in that approach is, if you're not careful, you can risk presenting Christianity as simply a code of ethics: if we all worked that little bit harder at following Jesus' commands (tried really hard to love our enemies, turn the other cheek, etc.), then the world would be a better place. No doubt it would, but the problem is all of us fail to live up to our own standards, let alone Jesus'. But thankfully, Jesus welcomes us— mess, brokenness, and all—which is one reason why the church sometimes goes wrong. Indeed, given that the church is full to the brim with broken people, it's a wonder things don't go badly wrong more often. There are no entry criteria for the church, and that, in an age of judgementalism, is maybe something we need to stress more often. As one friend who was struggling with faith once said to me, "What holds me back from becoming a Christian is I worry I'm not good enough for God. If Jesus knew what I was *really* like, he'd want nothing to do with me." I did my best to gently reassure this person that God knows *exactly* what we're like and still came and died for us in the person of Jesus. That we're not good enough is precisely the point.

Character and Boldness

But one last and crucial thought on all of this. Remember that the goal is not simply to be a *nice* person. After all, it is possible (indeed, worryingly easy) to be so concerned that our friends and colleagues *like* us so they will have a good impression of Christians that we try to be nice, charming, generous, and kind *instead* of sharing Christ, rather than doing this *alongside* sharing Christ, as the Bible exhorts us to do.

It is at this point that somebody will often raise their hand, cough politely like a badger choking on a toffee, and attempt to introduce into the conversation a famous quote frequently attributed to St. Francis of Assisi: "Preach the gospel at all times, and if necessary use words."

Back in my Undercover Christian days I remember stumbling across this quote, probably printed in Comic Sans font beneath one of those overly saturated landscape photos that often adorn Christian motivational posters. *Aha!* I thought. *It's okay that I'm timid and quiet about my faith because look, a famous saint was too. It's easy, it's Assisi!*

But there's a problem. Aside from the fact that, according to tradition, Francis spent much of his time hanging out with wildlife, and if you're preaching to the birds, a packet of seed is going to go further than a long-winded sermon,[10] the bigger issue is that Francis never said those words. The quote is a myth, a misattribution, one that has birthed a million memes that have spread as widely as that famous quote by Einstein: "Never trust anything you read on the Internet." Whilst Francis was famous for living a life of simplicity and compassion, he was also a tireless and fearless preacher—even walking into the wild parties thrown by the rich and preaching the gospel in the middle of them.

Your goal is not simply to be winsome and leave it there. Rather,

---

10 Although "tern the other cheek" might be a suitable text.

you want to aim to be winsome so that you might win some.[11] When we combine words and winsomeness, when we give a reason for the hope that we have and do this *with* gentleness and respect, God often works through this in amazing ways.

A few years ago, I was helping a group of students at a major Canadian university organise a week of outreach events on campus. During the planning, one student suggested doing a dialogue event with the leading LGBT group on campus. Not fully sure whether this was a brilliant idea or complete insanity, we extended the invitation and they accepted. For the Christian side, we invited my friend Sam Allberry, well known as a same-sex attracted Christian who is living a biblically faithful life.[12] On the evening of the event, as Sam dialogued with the president of the LGBT group, the lecture hall was filled to capacity, and you could have heard a pin drop. But time after time, Sam was able to graciously answer questions and challenges and repeatedly brought the conversation back to Jesus, explaining that his choosing to follow the Bible's teaching on sexuality was not a negative thing, because sexual intimacy is not the greatest thing we can experience. The greatest thing, the thing we're designed for, is intimacy with Christ, something on offer for all of us, no matter our sexual orientation. Sam's gentleness, grace, and generosity won the crowd over to him that evening.

But what showed us the impact that words matched with character can have was the email we received a few days later from the president of the LGBT group. She wrote to thank the Christian campus group for organising the event and went on to say how,

---

11 I have my friend Sarah Yardley, whom we met in chapter 4, to thank for that little catchphrase.
12 See, for example, Sam Allberry, *Is God Anti-Gay? And Other Questions about Homosexuality, the Bible, and Same-Sex Attraction* (Epsom, UK: Good Book Company, 2015).

before the evening, she had written off all Christians as homophobic bigots. "But Sam entirely changed my view, and I'm sorry for misjudging an entire community," she wrote. "Thank you for organising the event—and we'd love to welcome Sam to speak to us anytime he's back in this part of Canada."

Nobody is unreachable with the gospel. None of our friends or colleagues are beyond Jesus' ability to engage them. And in a world of division and tribalism, suspicion and judgementalism, people *are* looking for authenticity and are drawn to it when they see it. May we be people whose lives and words align—not afraid to speak up, nor afraid to show compassion, even at the cost of comfort and reputation. That's the way to overcome the church's reputation for crunchiness.

CHAPTER 15

FOOLISH EVANGELISM

I LOVE THE GREAT OUTDOORS, especially the mountains, and spend any time that I can spare hiking and climbing in them. I therefore own gargantuan quantities of hiking equipment, and one of my favourite pieces of kit is my ice axe. It hangs on my garage wall, amidst dozens of other tools, but stands out amongst them like a shark in a goldfish tank. Made of burnished steel that catches the light, it looks epic, it looks serious, and to my mind it says that its owner is a rugged adventurous type who could teach Bear Grylls a thing or two. However, there is just one little problem. I've never used the thing, other than one ill-fated attempt to open a wine bottle after we'd misplaced the corkscrew.[1] For some reason, I can't walk past an outdoor equipment shop without buying something,

---

[1] We're still finding bits of glass two years on.

usually a gadget of some kind, and so the garage is cluttered with myriad types of trekking poles, self-lighting camping stoves that don't, solar-powered snow goggles, and old tents for which we only have the instructions in Korean.

When it comes to my ice axe, I certainly *aspire* to use it, I *mean* to use it, I *plan* to use it. One day. Just not today. And meanwhile I regularly watch videos of other people doing epic things in the snow whilst the spiders in the garage use the ice axe as a major supporting pillar of the arachnid version of the Hanging Gardens of Babylon they're building up in the rafters.

It's one thing to buy a piece of kit. It's another to actually *use* it. And I want to suggest the same goes for books on evangelism. It's great that you've bought or borrowed this book and very encouraging that you have read as far as the final chapter. But I'm also aware that reading can for some of us be a displacement activity.[2] Back in my Undercover Christian days, I went through a phase when I read a shedload of books on evangelism, and after each I would tell myself, *I just need to read one more, then I'll be ready.* The simple fact is there are always more books to read and more things to learn, so there comes a time when we need to stop preparing and actually get started.

I hope you've learnt a lot from the last fourteen chapters. I hope you've realised you're not alone in finding evangelism hard; have been encouraged by some of the stories I've shared; have looked at some of the ideas, tools, and conversation starters and thought, *Maybe I could do that.* But now I'd like to encourage you to put the book into practice—to take the ice axe off the wall, as it were, and give it a swing. On the other hand, since waving sharp steel tools around the room is perhaps not the best metaphor for

---

[2] My wife pointed this out after I'd bought and read the fourth variation on *Ways to Organise a Messy Garage.*

evangelism,[3] let me offer you instead thirteen simple and practical ways to get started.

Thirteen Ways to Get Started in Evangelism

First, try praying. Specifically, I suggest praying for *opportunities*, that the Lord might bring people across your path (or to your attention). This sounds so obvious, but it's something I confess I regularly forget to do. One helpful trick that works for me is to put a little reminder on a Post-it Note and stick it somewhere I'll see it first thing in the morning—on the fridge, the kettle, or the cat. Seriously, psychologists will tell you that one of the best ways to learn a *new* habit is to connect it to an *existing* habit, so if the first thing you do each morning is boil the cat or put the kettle out, why not take a minute or two to pray whilst you're waiting for your first caffeine shot of the day to be ready?

Second, and sticking with the prayer theme, it can be really helpful to make a list of four or five non-Christians in your life—perhaps friends or colleagues—and try to create a habit of praying for them regularly. Daily is great, but don't beat yourself up if you fail to do that. What you want to do is create a prayer pattern that you can stick to. I've found writing a list and using it as a bookmark in my Bible is helpful.

Third, be brave and plant a faith flag at work or among friends. (We met this idea in chapter 4.) Maybe next time the "What did you do on the weekend?" question comes up in a conversation, don't pretend to have a furball-induced coughing fit, but say something really positive about church. Or bring an interesting Christian book to work and read it during the lunch break and

---

3 Look out for the sequel to this book, *How to Share Your Faith without Causing Head Injuries*, coming soon to a prison library near you.

be ready when colleagues ask what you're reading. Epic Christian biographies like Eric Liddell's or Corrie ten Boom's are super helpful here, as the stories of these kinds of folks are packed full of adventure as well as faith and can be easy talking points.[4]

Fourth, prayerfully consider what opportunities there might be to engage in a few random acts of kindness. For example, during the first COVID-19 lockdown in the UK in 2020, we bought Easter eggs for lots of local houses and delivered them on Easter Sunday, along with a little card, which was clearly Christian but not *cheesy* (nor, indeed, crunchy). If a colleague is having a tough time at work, could you leave a gift on their desk? Could you offer to take the neighbours' kids for an hour or two so they can get some rest one weekend? And remember, the key thing is not just to be a randomly nice person but when your neighbour or colleague asks, "Why did you do that?" to be bold and say, in your own words, that as a follower of Jesus, you're keen to find ways to show his love in action.

Fifth, look for an opportunity to have a worldview conversation. In chapter 5, I suggested there are four helpful questions we can ask friends who have either a different faith or no faith. Here they are again:

- Do you think there's some kind of god, and if so, what is god like?
- What does it mean to be a human being?
- What's gone wrong with the world?
- What's the solution?

---

[4] By the way, if you have kids, take the time to introduce them to Christian biographies as it can be terrifically exciting for young believers to get familiar with heroes of the past. I can highly recommend the Christian Heroes: Then & Now series by Janet and Geoff Benge. See www.ywampublishing.com/p-470-christian-heroes-then-nowbrcomplete-set-books-1-50.aspx.

So look for a chance to ask these. If, for example, you have a colleague who is a Muslim, why not grab lunch with them sometime and during the conversation say something like "I hope you don't mind me asking, but you're a Muslim—I don't know much about what Muslims believe; would you mind if I asked you a few questions?" And then you're away. With a friend who is an atheist, you might try setting up the discussion this way: "I've been reading a book on how to have better conversations about our deepest beliefs—I know you don't believe in God, but would you mind if I asked you some questions about what you *do* believe?" And then you can move on to the second, third, and fourth questions on the list above.

Sixth, use the *wondering* question we learnt in chapter 10 to start a spiritual conversation with a friend or colleague. Prayerfully look for places where they express an interest, desire, or passion that you think makes *more* sense if God is real. For example, perhaps you've gone for a hike with a friend and you're standing on the summit admiring the view. Rather than talk about the amazing new ice axe you've just nailed to the garage wall, you could remark, "Have you ever *wondered* why as humans we're so drawn to natural beauty and amazing landscapes?" Opportunities for good *wondering* questions are everywhere—in everyday life, in the movies we watch, and so on—so look out for them, make a note of them, and then weave them into conversations.

Seventh, share something on social media. Now, care is needed here, because in my humble opinion, the social media feeds of many Christians fall into one of two categories. Either we share *nothing* about faith, gumming up our feeds with pictures of our kids looking cute or the latest comedy meme that, let's be honest, everybody else already saw three years ago. Or some of us go the other way, plastering our social media with insanely naff Christian content or Christian conspiracy theories.[5] But there is a better way: namely, maintaining a relatively normal social media presence but dropping in good quality, thought-provoking Christian content regularly, the kind that your non-Christian friends and colleagues might be willing to watch. If you're stuck for ideas, have a look at some of the short videos and articles we regularly post at the Solas website.[6]

Eighth, try some hospitality. It's one of the most overlooked forms of pre-evangelism. Find opportunities to invite neighbours or colleagues for meals and then prayerfully look for ways to sow conversation starters into those times together. A friend of mine recently plucked up the courage to invite a Muslim colleague and his wife to dinner. The couple accepted, they had a lovely meal together, and the conversation soon turned to faith. But my friend was struck by something his Muslim colleague said at the end: "I have so enjoyed our evening. Thank you for inviting me and sharing what you believe. Do you know, I have lived in the UK for twenty years, and tonight was the first time I have been inside a Christian home."

Ninth, offer to pray for a friend. This can sometimes feel scary but can often be a real door opener to spiritual conversations. If a neighbour or friend has shared with you that they're struggling with something, be brave and consider asking if they'd mind if you prayed for them. You'll be amazed how often the answer is yes and how that simple offer of prayer can sometimes be the first step to deeper conversations.

---

5 Or conspiracy theories in general. If a non-Christian friend looks on your Facebook page and sees an article on the resurrection sandwiched between others on why vaccines cause country and western music, or why cell phone towers cause hair loss in tortoises, then your friend will probably conclude that the evidence for the resurrection is up there (or down there) with the evidence for the other things.

6 See, for example, www.solas-cpc.org/shortanswers/ or www.solas-cpc.org/hyew/.

Tenth, get involved with what your church is doing. Many pastors report that it can be tough getting people involved with evangelism, so make their lives easy for them. Volunteer to help at the Alpha course or whatever it is your church is doing. And if your church *isn't* doing anything particularly evangelistic, quite possibly it's because your poor pastor tried to start something and drummed up about as much interest as a hot dog stand at a vegan convention. So why not ask your church leader about starting something evangelistic and say you're willing not just to be involved but to recruit others?

Eleventh, if you're a parent, talk about the ideas in this book with your kids. So many young Christian students I meet are desperate for help and suggestions on sharing their faith at school or on campus, so make evangelism a family affair. Teach them some of the ideas and questions for good conversations, encourage them to try them out, celebrate with them when things go well, support them when things go wrong, and above all help them get a vision for sharing their faith at a young age. As somebody once remarked, "Youth was made for heroism, not for pleasure."

Twelfth, get inspired by what others are doing. If there are people in your church who are more naturally gifted at evangelism than you, spend time with them and get excited about what God is doing—and maybe learn some new ideas. Or dig into the many stories on the Solas website of Christians sharing their faith at work.[7] If there are other believers in your workplace, seek them out and get connected—it's easier to start praying for or reaching your workplace or campus if you're connected to others.

Thirteenthly (which is not a word you often hear these days,

7 See www.solas-cpc.org/frontlines/.

and hopefully never in a sermon), share this book with other Christian friends and start meeting, talking about it, and praying together. Evangelism is much easier when you know that others are holding you up in prayer.

Prayer Puts Jesus at the Centre of Evangelism

I hope that among the ideas on that list were some suggestions that made you think, *I could do that.* But I also hope you noticed something important: the list is bookended by prayer. I am constantly struck by how easy it is to slide into thinking that evangelism is all about me—my efforts, my fears, my failures, my successes, my mastery of a technique or a method, my ability to ask good questions.

As a boy, I was always fascinated by aviation, and one of my childhood memories is looking up each afternoon about 5:00 p.m. as Concorde, the supersonic passenger jet, flew over our house. When Concorde was retired from service and the remaining aircraft turned into museum pieces, I took the chance to visit the Aerospace Bristol museum, where in a hangar all to herself, beautifully lit and presented, is Concorde Alpha Foxtrot, the last of the Concordes to fly. Visitors are able to go on board, and as we walked through the first-class cabin, I was struck by something that was unique to Concorde—a Mach speed indicator at the front of the cabin, so passengers could see when they had broken the sound barrier. A friend who had regularly flown on Concorde told me that often the indicator would hover for a long time around Mach 0.9, as the pilots weren't allowed to break the sound barrier over land. Passengers would sometimes get up and tap the display, so keen were they for it to show the magic "Mach 1.0" figure. But of course, you couldn't change the speed of the plane by fiddling with the gauge, nor by willpower, nor by asking your fellow passengers to stand up and flap their arms. Only the pilots in the cockpit, by pushing on the throttle, could take Concorde through the sound barrier.[8]

It's the same when it comes to evangelism. We can put in all the effort we like, but unless we're connected to the source of the power, we're going to be frustrated. And this is why prayer is so crucial. It reminds us whose work evangelism ultimately is—and it keeps us connected to the Holy Spirit, the one who can move the throttles of the hearts and minds we long to reach and make them receptive.

Sometimes prayer and aviation can come together in more than just a metaphor. I remember receiving an email from Millie, a woman who, along with her husband, had attended an evangelism seminar at a conference I was speaking at. They worked for another Christian ministry and were running a stand in the exhibition at the conference. After the seminar, she had prayed that the Lord might open up an opportunity for her to use some of what she'd learnt. Her email told what happened next:

> After the conference, we had to catch a flight to Scotland, where we were exhibiting at another conference. Normally when we fly, Neil [her husband] ends up in the middle seat next to a stranger, and he has all kind of amazing conversations, while I'm stuck on the aisle. But on this occasion, British Airways had messed up our booking, so we were seated many rows apart. I got chatting to the woman next to me and in the course of our conversation,

---

[8] Thanks to Gavin Matthews for this illustration.

she asked why I'd been in Bristol. I said I'd been at a
conference. "What kind of conference?" she asked. I said
it was a Christian conference and instantly she became
very prickly, muttering something about how she didn't
have any time for religion. Normally I'd have had no idea
what to say next, but remembering your session, I smiled
sweetly and said, "I'm really sorry to have upset you;
why do you say that?" Well, that opened up the whole
conversation—I think because I wasn't defensive or angry
at what she'd said—and I discovered how she'd had a
really bad experience with church as a teenager. We talked
about that, and I was able in due course to ask what
she thought about Jesus, and we even exchanged email
addresses at the end. When I prayed that afternoon for
opportunities, I had no idea that God would answer my
prayer within a few hours.

Notice that Millie's conversation didn't end with her fellow passenger having a weeping conversion there on the airplane, press-
ing the call button, and asking the flight attendant to bring a few
dozen bottles of water so they could do an impromptu baptism.
Does that make Millie's conversation a failure in some way? I think
for some of us that is another of those fears that can cripple us
from sharing our faith with confidence. *What happens if I share
my faith with a friend, neighbour, or colleague and nothing happens?*
Please don't mistake this for flippancy, but my initial response
is, *What's the problem, precisely?* First, of course, how can you be
sure that "nothing" happened? You've no idea what's happening
on the inside, and over the years I've often been surprised to see
people come to faith in Christ who I'd assumed were so far from

the gospel they couldn't see it with a telescope on a clear day. There are biblical examples of this. Who could have expected Saul to become a Jesus follower? Or Nicodemus? Whilst he was creeping around at night, secretly meeting Jesus for conversations, presumably during the day he gave all the outward signs of being just another Pharisee.

We also forget that even giants of the Bible had experiences and encounters where things did not always go swimmingly. Think of Paul, for example, driven out of town after town or preaching his heart out and seeing just a few respond. Or think of Jesus, who in the Parable of the Sower forewarned us that there would be plenty of times when the seed fell in all the wrong places. And in Mark 6, Jesus visits his hometown, where his own people pour scorn on him and he is able to do very few miracles because of their lack of faith. Perhaps biblical examples like this remind us that what God is asking of us is not success but faithfulness, not ability but availability. So be encouraged. Whatever happens as we fulfil Jesus' command to "go and make disciples," we have his accompanying promise: "Surely I am with you always, to the very end of the age."[9]

You can also draw comfort from the fact that it has been estimated that it often takes a dozen or more encounters with different Christians for somebody to come to faith in Christ. It is rare that a total non-Christian bumps into a Christian, has one conversation, and then boom! becomes a follower of Jesus. What is far more the norm is that as somebody meets several Christians and has different conversations—sometimes over many years—the Holy Spirit works in their hearts.

---

9 Matthew 28:19-20.

Try imagining a scale from 1 to 100, with 1 representing somebody as far from God as it is possible to be, short of them upping sticks and moving to 668 Babylon Avenue,[10] The City of Destruction, whilst 100 signifies somebody who has just given their life to Christ for the first time. When you're talking about Jesus with your friend, have in mind that your task—as Christ's ambassador, relying on prayer and the Holy Spirit—is simply to move them up that scale. Maybe God will use you to move your friend from 2 to 17. A year later, somebody else will be used to move them into the 30s, and so on. Thinking of evangelism this way means we can rejoice when we see any glimpse of the Holy Spirit at work in somebody's life through our speaking with them. The apostle Paul makes a similar point:

> What, after all, is Apollos? And what is Paul? Only
> servants, through whom you came to believe—as the Lord
> has assigned to each his task. I planted the seed, Apollos
> watered it, but God has been making it grow. So neither
> the one who plants nor the one who waters is anything,
> but only God, who makes things grow. The one who
> plants and the one who waters have one purpose, and they
> will each be rewarded according to their own labour. For
> we are fellow workers in God's service; you are God's field,
> God's building.
>
> I CORINTHIANS 3:5-9

It can also be helpful to think back to your own path to faith in Christ. If you're like me, it may very well be the case that several

---

10 668 being, of course, the neighbour of the Beast.

people were involved. In my case, I'm grateful to my parents, to several youth leaders, and to one or two key Christian friends, all of whom took the time to pray for me, talk about faith with me, answer my questions, show what Christian love and generosity looks like in action, and explain why Jesus is worth following. If you simply asked me, "When did you become a Christian?" one answer is certainly "When I walked forward at a youth camp meeting, in a tent on a dark and stormy night on the cliffs above Hastings on the south coast of England." But the truth is that the message the youth leader preached that evening wasn't particularly impressive. Rather, that was the point at which the Holy Spirit drew all those other threads together. Think back to your own conversion and all the people involved, and be encouraged that the Lord can use you in the same way.

But what if it is our privilege to be there when somebody arrives at the finishing line, when somebody is ready to commit their life to following Christ? That's another fear I know can hold some of us back. What do we say? Is there a magic prayer formula that if we don't get quite right, this person's whole Christian life will go wrong? Well, be encouraged, because when we read through the New Testament, two things are striking. First, there *are* no magic formulae. And second, the first Christians tended to go for simplicity and clarity. Here's Paul again: "If you declare with your mouth, 'Jesus is Lord,' and believe in your heart that God raised him from the dead, you will be saved."[11]

And here's Peter, after the very first recorded sermon in Christian history (in which, thankfully, he didn't get anywhere near "thirteenthly"): " Repent and be baptised, every one of you,

---

[11] Romans 10:9.

in the name of Jesus Christ for the forgiveness of your sins. And you will receive the gift of the Holy Spirit."[12]

Over the years, I've learnt so much from others on how to do this, and now, when offering to pray with somebody who is ready to follow Jesus, I encourage them to formulate a prayer around three words: sorry, thanks, and please. "I'm *sorry*, Lord, that I've lived my life as a rebel and ignored and rejected you. *Thanks* for your love, kindness, and forgiveness and for Jesus' death and resurrection that make that possible. *Please*, would you fill me with your Holy Spirit, make me a new creation, and empower me to start following Jesus from now on?"

Everyday Evangelism

As I mentioned earlier, I have noticed over the years that books on evangelism sometimes leave us feeling a bit daunted. Much as I love testimonies and missionary stories, much as I love books full of clever techniques, sometimes I would end up feeling *What a shame I can't be like Hudson Taylor* or *How I wish I could remember step 17 of that programme.* But I've come to realise that the *best* evangelism, the most *effective* evangelism, is simply evangelism that is woven into everyday life. Especially in a culture that wants to turn religion into a private thing, where many of our friends think Christianity has nothing meaningful to say about their lives, evangelism that is woven into the everyday worlds of work, school, family, and friends is ultimately going to have more impact. As we are in contact with our colleagues and friends, as we naturally let our faith in Christ shine out in our conversations, that's when the Holy Spirit can work most effectively.

---

[12] Acts 2:38.

How do we avoid looking like an idiot? Well, it seems to me that the opposite of being an idiot is to be *wise*. And that's what I've tried to do—sometimes more successfully, occasionally less so—since my Undercover Christian days. I've learnt from others who share their faith more easily than me; I've put the time into finding some very simple, basic tools that can help in conversations; I've tried to daily remind myself to pray—and then pray some more; I've sought for and grabbed hold of opportunities as the Lord sends them; and I've learnt to take risks (and not worry when things go wrong). And in all of this, I've held these words of the Bible front and centre:

> Be wise in the way you act towards outsiders; make the most of every opportunity. Let your conversation be always full of grace, seasoned with salt, so that you may know how to answer everyone.
>
> COLOSSIANS 4:5-6

A few years ago, I was helping to lead a week of mission at a large Canadian university. Several of the campus groups had come together to put on five days of lunchtime and evening talks, with guest speakers addressing a range of common questions about the Christian faith. Each morning we would start with a prayer meeting and encourage the students to invite friends to the day's events. One particular girl, Li, a fairly young Christian, explained that she was too afraid to invite her classmates or roommates to any of the events. "What if they say no or maybe don't want to be friends with me afterward?" she fretted. Finally, after a few days of encouragement from her Christian friends, Li eventually plucked up the courage to ask someone from her maths class to come to the talk that lunchtime, where a local pastor was speaking on the nicely controversial topic "Why Does God Care What We Do in the Bedroom?" To Li's complete and utter surprise, her friend said yes to the invitation, came to the event, and even asked a couple of questions in the Q and A after the talk. She then hung around and spoke with the pastor for three hours, after which he and Li were able to pray with her to become a Christian.

At the following morning's prayer meeting, I have never seen anybody so rapidly grown in confidence. From a shy, quiet person who rarely said a word, Li had undergone a transformation. As she shared with her fellow students, "I never, ever, ever thought God could use *me*. But yesterday he used me to lead my friend to Jesus! I would never have believed I could be an evangelist."

Your own experience as you read and apply this book may not be quite so dramatic as Li's. But I have seen—and experienced in my own life—that when we find our voice and speak up, God can use even the smallest and weakest of us for his purposes. I hope this book may help you towards that discovery too.

Jesus does not ask us to look like idiots. But he does ask us to be foolish and to take a risk. In doing so, he does not ask us to do anything he has not already done himself. Indeed, that he has not done *first*. For in Jesus, God took the risk, took the initiative, gave his all, stepping into history, knowing full well what it would cost him. And God did this because of his tremendous love for us *and* his great love for our friends.

And thus, the good news is that however much we want to share the gospel with our friends and colleagues, however great our desire is for them to know Jesus, God's desire is infinitely bigger than ours, proven by what he did in Jesus. God's love for our friends is far, far greater than ours. And so, as we step out in faith, we do this not in our power, but in the power of the Holy Spirit that God gives us. As the Bible puts it so beautifully:

> Now to him who is able to do immeasurably more than all we ask or imagine, according to his power that is at work within us, to him be glory in the church and in Christ Jesus throughout all generations, for ever and ever! Amen.
>
> EPHESIANS 3:20-21

ACKNOWLEDGEMENTS

A LONG TIME AGO IN A GALAXY FAR, FAR AWAY . . . Well, actually it was 2012, and it was only Winnipeg (although even to Canadians, that can sometimes feel like Andromeda). So much for epic scene setting—it wasn't even a dark and stormy night, but it was, as I recall, a weekend of azure blue skies and wall-to-wall sunshine, although it *was* negative 45° Celsius.[1]

I'd been invited by a large missions conference to run a seminar on practical, everyday evangelism. "But we can't just call it that," said one of the organisers on the group planning call. "We need a zippy title."

"'Lighting the Fires of Evangelism'?" I suggested.

"I said *zippy*, not *Zippo*. Besides, that's also a rubbish title."

I explained that titles are really not my strong point,[2] and so over the next thirty minutes the four of us on the call brainstormed some ideas. Finally, somebody suggested, "What about 'How to Talk about Jesus without Looking like an Idiot'?" and there was much rejoicing. We ran the seminar with that name, it was hugely

---

[1] They breed them tough in Winnipeg, and those who have the misfortune to be bred floppy freeze solid soon enough.

[2] My first popular book on atheism I had planned to call *Why Sweden Doesn't Exist—and Other Curious Problems for Atheism*, until the publisher patiently explained, with diagrams, that this was way too surreal.

oversubscribed, and in the ten years since, I must have used that
title almost a hundred times, whenever I've taught this material. I
think it works so well because it names the elephant in the room.
Frankly, it names it Dumbo, which is what so many of us are afraid
of being called (or worse) if we try evangelism.

Fast forward to 2021, and I had just finished writing my
previous book, *Do Muslims and Christians Worship the Same
God?* (it turns out that a pandemic and associated lockdowns
remove any excuse for being too busy to write, or indeed for
painting the shelves one's wife has been asking about for four
years). The ink still wet on the manuscript,[3] my long-suffering
agent, Mark, rang me up to ask if I had any ideas for the next
book. I brushed him off with an excuse along the lines of "I can't
speak right now; I'm about to address a room full of people on
how to talk about Jesus without looking like an idiot." "That's
the next book!" Mark exclaimed. And he was right. Since I had
been speaking on this title for ten years, it was time to write it
as a book.

In many ways, this is very much the third book in a trilogy.
The first two—*The Atheist Who Didn't Exist* and *Do Muslims and
Christians Worship the Same God?*—were aimed *outside* the church,
at those of no faith or of a very different faith. I've been hugely
encouraged to see where they've landed and the conversations
they've started. One guy emailed me to say he'd been on vacation with his atheist sister, who'd seen the cover of *The Atheist
Who Didn't Exist* and had been intrigued, picked it up, and then
read it through over the next few days, laughing out loud and
quoting bits. He wrote, "For the last twenty years, the door to

---

[3] That'll teach me to buy a cheap inkjet printer.

conversations with her about faith has been nailed shut. But that book opened the door—just a chink, but it's now open." Another person emailed to say how *Do Muslims and Christians Worship the Same God?* had helped her have really fruitful conversations about Jesus with her Muslim daughter-in-law.

But this third book is aimed at Christians, and I hope it will help you start conversations with friends, neighbours, and colleagues for which, in time, the other two books may also be a great resource (and gift). One common thread running through all three books is *comedy*. In each, I've made (faltering and imperfect) attempts to weave humour and laughter into the text (and the footnotes—don't forget to read the footnotes!).

Humour can be very powerful. It helps build a connection, it can lower our defences so we're more willing to consider ideas we might find challenging or subversive, and it also, above all, connects directly to the imagination like a metal spoon shoved into an electric socket. Too often Christians have forgotten the power of the imagination. We're quick in our evangelism to connect to the mind, even to the heart, but it's the *imagination* that we also need to reach if people are to see the Good News as compelling. (Of course, there's a "Have you ever wondered?" question here, too, isn't there? I wonder why it is we find humour so compelling? There's a question to ask a friend next time you're roaring with laughter at a joke or some TV sitcom.)

Most of my own comedy influences were not Christian ones (with the possible exception of Adrian Plass, who deserves to be far better known on the American side of the Atlantic). People like Terry Pratchett, the Pythons, or Douglas Adams, among many others, have left quite a mark on me. Speaking of Adams, I was recently leafing through his classic *The Hitch Hiker's Guide to the*

Galaxy and discovered he had written something that quickly became a metaphor for what I was trying to do with this book:

> In many of the more relaxed civilisations on the Outer
> Eastern Rim of the Galaxy, the *Hitch Hiker's Guide* has
> already supplanted the great *Encyclopaedia Galactica* as
> the standard repository of all knowledge and wisdom, for
> though it has many omissions and contains much that is
> apocryphal, or at least wildly inaccurate, it scores over the
> older, more pedestrian work in two important respects.
> First, it is slightly cheaper; and secondly it has the words
> DON'T PANIC inscribed in large friendly letters on its
> cover.[4]

I hope there is not *too* much in this book that is wildly inaccurate, or even apocryphal. But I do hope that "DON'T PANIC" is a theme running through it. Just as every intergalactic hitchhiker needs to know where their towel is, I hope if you're aspiring to share your faith with your friends, you'll always know where your copy of *How to Talk about Jesus without Looking like an Idiot* is.

Writing is not an easy process. In his classic poem "The Writer,"[5] Richard Wilbur uses the metaphor of a bird trapped in a room trying frantically to find its way to the open window to describe the endless effort of searching for the right word, phrase, or metaphor. Often as I struggle to write, I worry that the bird has snuffed it entirely and there's a need for a 12-volt battery and a set of jump leads, but I agree with Wilbur's conclusion in his poem: that writing is a matter of life or death. This is especially true of

---

4 Douglas Adams, *The Hitch Hiker's Guide to the Galaxy* (London: Pan Books, 1980), 7.
5 Read it online here: www.poets.org/poem/writer.

writing concerned with something so crucial as the gospel and how we share that Good News with those we care deeply about. I'm therefore hugely grateful to all my friends who encouraged me and prayed whilst I've worked on the book.

There are also, as always, some special thanks due. First, a massive thank you to my team of colleagues and friends at Solas, the ministry I have the privilege of leading in the UK. They've had to put up with my absences from meetings, distractedness, trying out one-liners to find what works, and a thousand and one ways in which I wasn't fully there at times. Thanks, all of you, for your support and enthusiasm for my writing. Thanks also to Michael Ots and Aaron Edwards for being sounding boards for so many ideas—and for sourdough recipes and Tolkien geekery.

Thanks also to my agent, Mark Sweeney, who probably has less hair than when this project began, but now it's done, can stop tearing it out and probably go wig shopping. Thanks, Mark, for your encouragement, hard work, and belief in this book when it was just a clever title.

And a massive shout-out to Jon Farrar, Jonathan Schindler, and the wonderful team at Tyndale, who have been simply amazing to work with. If they've had half as much fun editing this book as I had writing it, I'll have had twice as much fun as them. Seriously, as somebody once said, "There are no bad authors, only bad editors"—and their brilliant editing has made this book what it is.

Finally, a thank-you to my wife, Astrid, and my two children, Caitriona and Christopher. It's not easy being the family of an author, living with endless requests for quiet so concentration can happen or the regular thumping sounds of heads banging on desks when words won't behave. But I couldn't have written this book without your love and support—nor without the regular requests to leave the keyboard and come play Carcassonne or Exploding Kittens.[6] And above all I'm grateful to Jesus, for his kindness, grace, and patience—and for being willing to work through a weak and broken vessel like me. I hope this book has, as far as possible, kept the focus on him, not the writer. As the words of one of my favourite hymns put it,

> *O Lord, Thy heavenly grace impart,*
> *And fix my frail, inconstant heart;*
> *Henceforth my chief desire shall be*
> *To dedicate myself to Thee,*
> *To Thee, my God, to Thee.*
>
> *Whate'er pursuits my time employ,*
> *One thought shall fill my heart with joy:*
> *That silent, secret thought shall be,*
> *That all my hopes are fixed on Thee,*
> *On Thee, my God, on Thee.*[7]

---

[6] I think I may be the only writer who has managed to get Exploding Kittens into a book on evangelism and *Pride and Prejudice and Zombies* into a book on Islam.

[7] Written by Jean Frédéric Oberlin (1740–1826).

APPENDIX 1

A HANDY CUT-AND-KEEP GUIDE[1]

To HELP YOU PUT INTO PRACTISE the four questions I've taught in the heart of this book, as well as the five steps of SHARE, I have created this handy guide. Consider cutting out the sections below (if you're especially practical, you could even laminate the result). You can then slip them into your wallet or purse—that is, put them somewhere you'll regularly stumble across them—where they will then serve as a frequent reminder to use these very practical tools in everyday conversations.

---

[1] Scissors not included with this paperback due to health and safety concerns.

What?

Example: "What did you mean by the word *god*?"

Why?

Example: "Why do you think that all religions lead to god?"

Wondering?

**Example: "Have you ever wondered why
we're so drawn to art and beauty?"**

Whether?

**Example: "I wonder whether Christianity makes better
sense of human rights and dignity than the alternatives?"**

THAT REMINDS ME . . .

*. . . of something **Jesus said***

*. . . of something **Jesus did***

*. . . of a story **Jesus told***

THE FIVE STEPS OF SHARE

Sympathise

Build a connection and rapport with the person
asking the question.

Hidden assumptions

Help your friend see the things they haven't considered
in their own beliefs.

Apply the Bible

How does the question/objection look when you view
it from the cross?

Retell the gospel

Talk about Jesus through your answer to their
question.

Equip your friend

Leave your friend with a book, article, video, etc.,
to explore later.

BOOKS AND RESOURCES TO HELP YOU CONTINUE THE JOURNEY

HERE IS A USEFUL LIST OF RESOURCES to help you dig deeper into some of what we've covered in this book. It's broken down into three sections: first, a selection of free digital resources from Solas, the ministry I lead in the UK; second, some books designed to help you further develop your conversational evangelism skills (such as asking good questions); and third, a wide range of books tackling some of the common questions and objections that people have about Christianity.

Free Digital Resources

Frontlines: Christians Sharing Their Faith at Work
www.solas-cpc.org/frontlines/
How can we learn from others when it comes to sharing our faith at work? *Frontlines* is a series of interviews with Christians working in a wide range of jobs and industries, each of whom models for us different ways we can talk about the gospel with our colleagues.

Mind the Gap: Overcoming Everyday Barriers
to Sharing the Gospel
www.solas-cpc.org/gap/
In chapter 2 we explored some of the fears that keep us from talking about Jesus with confidence, but there are other gaps that often hold us back from evangelism. This helpful series addresses some of these and helps you continue to grow in boldness and confidence.

Have You Ever Wondered?
www.solas-cpc.org/hyew/
In this series of articles (and in many cases associated videos), we look at a huge range of *wondering*-type topics. These are perfect for sharing with your friends to start conversations, or for learning more about how to ask your own "Have you ever wondered?" questions.

Short Answers
www.solas-cpc.org/shortanswers/
This is a library of more than one hundred videos (aimed at non-Christians, so watch and share!). Each episode takes a common question about Christianity and tries to offer an answer, usually in about five minutes.

A Beginner's Guide to Apologetics
www.solas-cpc.org/bgta/
In chapter 12 we scratched the surface of apologetics and began to think about how to give an answer for our hope. In this series, we take a wide range of different arguments and evidence for

Christianity, explain them clearly, and help you understand how to use them in evangelism. Whether you're interested in science, suffering, or the resurrection, there's something here to help you talk more persuasively about Christ.

Conversational Evangelism Resources
(Talking about Jesus Naturally)

Gregory Koukl, *Tactics: A Game Plan for Discussing Your Christian Convictions*, 10th Anniversary Edition (Grand Rapids, MI: Zondervan, 2019).

Randy Newman, *Questioning Evangelism: Engaging People's Hearts the Way Jesus Did*, 2nd Edition (Grand Rapids, MI: Kregel, 2017).

Rebecca Manley Pippert, *Out of the Saltshaker and into the World: Evangelism as a Way of Life* (Downers Grove, IL: InterVarsity, 2021).

Doug Pollock, *God Space: Where Spiritual Conversations Happen Naturally* (Loveland, CO: Group Publishing, 2009).

General Apologetics Resources
(Giving a Reason for the Hope You Have)

Christopher Brooks, *Urban Apologetics: Why the Gospel Is Good News for the City* (Grand Rapids, MI: Kregel, 2014).

Rebecca McLaughlin, *Confronting Christianity: 12 Hard Questions for the World's Largest Religion* (Wheaton, IL: Crossway, 2019).

Chris Sinkinson, *Confident Christianity: Conversations That Lead to the Cross* (London: InterVarsity, 2010).

Help with a "Have You Ever Wondered?" Approach

Holly Ordway, *Apologetics and the Christian Imagination: An Integrated Approach to Defending the Faith* (Steubenville, OH: Emmaus Road Publishing, 2017).

Michael Ots, *Making Sense of Life* (Leyland, UK: 10Publishing, 2021).

Rick Stedman, *31 Surprising Reasons to Believe in God: How Superheroes, Art, Environmentalism, and Science Point toward Faith* (Eugene, OR: Harvest House, 2017).

Daniel Strange, *Plugged In: Connecting Your Faith with What You Watch, Read, and Play* (Epsom, UK: Good Book Company, 2019).

Faith and Suffering

Sharon Dirckx, *Why?: Looking at God, Evil and Personal Suffering* (London: InterVarsity, 2021).

Jeremy Marshall, *Beyond the Big C: Hope in the Face of Death* (Leyland, UK: 10Publishing, 2019).

Amy Orr-Ewing, *Where Is God in All the Suffering?* (Epsom, UK: Good Book Company, 2020).

Sexuality

Sam Allberry, *Is God Anti-Gay?: And Other Questions about Homosexuality, the Bible and Same-Sex Attraction* (Epsom, UK: Good Book Company, 2015).

David Bennett, *A War of Loves: The Unexpected Story of a Gay Activist Discovering Jesus* (Grand Rapids, MI: Zondervan, 2018).

Rosaria Champagne Butterfield, *The Secret Thoughts of an Unlikely Convert: An English Professor's Journey into Christian Faith* (Pittsburgh, PA: Crown & Covenant, 2012).

Ed Shaw, *Purposeful Sexuality: A Short Christian Introduction* (London: InterVarsity, 2021).

Science

Francis S. Collins, *The Language of God: A Scientist Presents Evidence for Belief* (New York: Simon & Schuster, 2007).

David Hutchings and Tom McLeish, *Let There Be Science: Why God Loves Science, and Science Needs God* (Oxford: Lion, 2017).

John C. Lennox, *Can Science Explain Everything?* (Epsom, UK: Good Book Company, 2019).

Islam and Other Faiths

Andy Bannister, *Do Muslims and Christians Worship the Same God?* (London: InterVarsity, 2021).

Ellis Potter, *3 Theories of Everything* (Huemoz, Switzerland: Destinée Media, 2012).

Nabeel Qureshi, *Seeking Allah, Finding Jesus: A Devout Muslim Encounters Christianity*, 3rd Edition (Grand Rapids, MI: Zondervan, 2018).

Christian History

John Dickson, *Bullies and Saints: An Honest Look at the Good and Evil of Christian History* (Grand Rapids, MI: Zondervan Reflective, 2021).

Tom Holland, *Dominion: The Making of the Western Mind* (New York: Basic Books, 2021).

Christianity and Culture

Lamin Sanneh, *Whose Religion Is Christianity?: The Gospel beyond the West* (Grand Rapids, MI: Eerdmans, 2003).

The Bible

Richard Bauckham, *Jesus and the Eyewitnesses: The Gospels as Eyewitness Testimony*, 2nd Edition (Grand Rapids, MI: Eerdmans, 2017).

Amy Orr-Ewing, *Why Trust the Bible?: Answers to 10 Tough Questions* (London: Inter Varsity, 2020).

Peter J. Williams, *Can We Trust the Gospels?* (Wheaton, IL: Crossway, 2018).

Jesus and the Resurrection

Gary R. Habermas and Michael R. Licona, *The Case for the Resurrection of Jesus* (Grand Rapids, MI: Kregel, 2004).

Rebecca Manley Pippert, *Discovering the Real Jesus* (Epsom, UK: Good Book Company, 2016).

N. T. Wright, *Simply Jesus: A New Vision of Who He Was, What He Did, and Why He Matters* (New York: HarperOne, 2011).

DISCUSSION GUIDE

1. Andy describes his experience of being a Christian at work: "I spent years feeling incredibly guilty for being afraid of my Christian faith at work, for burying it away, for role-playing Undercover Christian" (page 6). In what ways does Andy's experience resonate with you? What are some of your fears about being known as a Christian at work, at school, or among your circle of friends?

2. The fear of how others might respond to us if we share our faith can take six common forms: looking like an idiot or being disliked, standing out from the crowd, being called names, causing arguments or division, harming our career, and being asked a question we can't answer. Which of these fears do you deal with the most and why?

3. The apostle Peter writes, "Do not fear what they fear; do not be frightened. But in your hearts set apart Christ as Lord" (1 Peter 3:14-15). In scary situations, how can focusing on Christ as Lord help us work through our temptation to fear?

4. Peter continues, "Always be prepared to give an answer to everyone who asks you to give the reason for the hope that you have. But do this with gentleness and respect" (1 Peter 3:15-16). What does it mean to be prepared to share our faith? Why are gentleness and respect important as we talk with others?

5. Asking questions or sparking curiosity in others that encourages them to ask you questions can help start organic conversations about faith. What can we learn from Jesus' approach to asking questions as we consider how to talk to our friends about him?

6. "The *what* question is designed to unpack, challenge, or tease apart what somebody has said," Andy writes (page 98). Think of a time when the subject of faith came up in conversation. How could a *what* question have been used to deepen that conversation?

7. Think of a common objection to Christianity that you have heard a friend or colleague raise. What is a good *why* question that would challenge that person to think more deeply and perhaps start a spiritual conversation?

8. Andy writes, "Sometimes in the church we are tempted to neglect [giving the reason for our hope], or we lean towards giving how-shaped answers to why-shaped questions" (page 129). If someone asked you why you are a Christian, what would you say? What reasons (rather than a "how-shaped" testimony) might you give in response to this *why* question?

9. A *wondering* question encourages someone to think more deeply about something they care about and how it might

point towards the God of the Bible. What would be a good *wondering* questions to ask someone who cares about justice? Freedom? Family? Art? Another topic a friend of yours is passionate about?

10. Andy says that using the *what, why, wondering,* and *whether* questions in combination can be especially effective. "Through asking good questions, listening well, and creating space for spiritual conversations, we want to find the opportunity to invite people to consider *whether,* to 'Come and see!'" (page 163). Think about this model of talking about Jesus with the people you know. What do you like about this model? What do you find challenging?

11. When we are asked tough questions, Andy advises, "First, remember that our task is to answer the *questioner,* not the question. Behind every question, behind every objection to the gospel is an individual person, and that's who we want to reach" (page 168). As you answer someone's question, how can you communicate care for that person? What are some approaches that shut down the conversation or drive people away?

12. Andy suggests five steps for answering a tough question, represented by the acronym SHARE: sympathise, hidden assumptions, apply the Bible, retell the gospel story, and equip your friend (see pages 169–172). Think of a tough question or objection to Christianity you have heard. How might you answer that question using these five steps?

13. What are some misconceptions people have about Christianity that stem from preconceived notions about

religion? Why is it important in conversations with our friends to differentiate between religion and the gospel of Jesus? What are some ways we might do this?

14. Prayer is vital in the work of evangelism, connecting us to the Holy Spirit, who has the power to move hearts and minds. Who are four or five people who are not yet Christians whom you feel prompted to pray for? Write their names down, put the list somewhere you will see it often, and begin praying regularly for opportunities to start conversations about Jesus with them.

15. Andy writes, "What God is asking of us is not success but faithfulness, not ability but availability" (page 231). How does this statement encourage you? What would you like to ask God for as you take the next step in evangelism? Take a moment to pray and ask for his help.

ABOUT THE AUTHOR

ANDY BANNISTER is the director of Solas, a UK-based evangelistic organisation that takes the good news of Jesus out of the four walls of the church and into the public square and also trains and equips Christians to talk naturally and winsomely about their faith.

A popular speaker (everywhere from universities to cafés to TV and radio), Andy is also the author of several books, including *Do Muslims and Christians Worship the Same God?* and *The Atheist Who Didn't Exist, Or: The Dreadful Consequences of Bad Arguments*.

Andy has been married for twenty-four years to his wife, Astrid, and they have two energetic, creative children, Caitriona and Christopher. When not writing, speaking, or broadcasting, Andy climbs mountains, chops wood, drinks tea, collects old books, and gets thoroughly clobbered by his kids at board games.

ANDY BANNISTER is the director of Solas, an evangelism and training ministry based in the United Kingdom. He regularly speaks in the United Kingdom, North America, and further afield for churches and organisations both large and small. So if you've enjoyed *How to Talk about Jesus without Looking like an Idiot* and would like to invite Andy to speak at your church or event, you can easily find him online by searching for "Andy Bannister Solas" or "Andy Bannister speaker."